SCALING YOUR EVEREST

Lessons From Sir Edmund Hillary

Lessons From Sir Edmund Hillary

James O. Davis

Cutting Edge International
Orlando, Florida

Unless otherwise indicated, all Scripture quotations are taken from the New American Standard Bible, copyright © The Lockman Foundation 1960, 1962, 1963, 1968, 1971, 1972, 1973, 1975, 1977, 1995. Used by permission.

Scaling Your Everest: Lessons From Sir Edmund Hillary

Cutting Edge International
Orlando, Florida

ISBN: 978-0-9887884-5-9

Copyright © 2013 James O. Davis

James O. Davis
P. O. Box 411605
Melbourne, Florida 32941

www.JamesODavis.com

DEDICATED TO

My Incredible Dad,
James W. Davis,
Who Climbed His Mountains,
Raised Two Godly Sons,
Laid To Rest A Gorgeous Wife
And Is Helping His Mother To Finish Her Race!

Table of Contents

The Big Decision   9

Question One:
How Can I Become A Focused Man?   19

Question Two:
What Is Life's Greatest Satisfaction?   39

Question Three:
How Can I Overcome Life's Greatest Obstacles?   59

Question Four:
When Should I Get Started?   75

Conclusion:
The Greatest Loss In A Man's Life   91

1

The Big Decision

Sir Edmund Hillary is generally considered to be the last great explorer of the twentieth century. He was the one who first reached the summit of Mt. Everest, scaling it in 1953.

I remember when I first heard of Sir Edmund Hillary. I was attending seminary and just starting out in ministry. On a Monday night, I was invited to minister at a First Assembly of God church in northern Indiana. I planned to speak on Isaac and Abraham. At the time, I was also reading about how Sir Edmund Hillary climbed Everest. Edmund Hillary had gone where no one had gone before. I was thinking about how Abraham took his son up a mountain out of obedience to God, going where no one had ever gone before. There was a spiritual parallel in these two great adventurers.

That Monday night started some months of research and a lifelong admiration. I read about Sir Edmund Hillary's climb on Mt. Everest in 1953. I read one author who wrote about how Sir Edmund tried to summit in 1952 but failed to conquer the mountain. Many trained climbers had tried to make it up the mountain and failed. Even if they got partway up, they failed on the descent.

When Sir Edmund trekked back down, he was laughed at by some and openly mocked by others. Who was he, trying to do what no one had ever done? He was just an ordinary beekeeper!

At the press conference held for Sir Edmund about his experience, he surprised everyone. He hung a large picture of Everest on the wall behind him. Some of the reporters took the opportunity to remind him, "It's not possible to climb Mt. Everest. Even if you could get to the top, you could not live there. You would surely die on the top or die on your way back down. Half of the battle is getting up, the other half is getting back down."

The young Edmund Hillary stood in front of that audience and said, "Look at the picture of Mt. Everest behind me."

Then he said, "I want you to see how large it is. I want you to see how wide it is. Mt. Everest stopped growing a long time ago but Edmund Hillary hasn't stopped growing yet. A year from today, I will climb to the top of Mt. Everest and I will hoist high the British flag and I will stand where no one has ever stood before."

A year later, on May 29, 1953, Edmund Hillary did it. He stood on what he aptly called the "Roof of the World."

As men with many decisions ahead of us, we need to realize that a vision only becomes a goal when we put a date to it. Edmund Hillary could have said, "Someday I'm going to climb to the top. Someday I'll go and stand where no one has stood. Someday I think I'll try to do this." Instead he became very specific and very strategic. He declared, "A year from today, I will climb to the top of Mt. Everest, I will hoist high the British Flag and I will stand where no one has ever stood before."

After reading his story, I could not get Sir Edmund's profound statement out of my heart. *The mountain has stopped growing, but I am still growing!*

For twenty-five years, when the thought of that feat and Sir Edmund would come to me, I would pray for him. From afar, I watched how he lived. Even with his fame, Sir Edmund was a very giving and gracious man. He helped raise money from around the world for the people who lived in the Himalayan Mountains. He was known for the schools that he started and the airports he founded in that region of the world.

In August of 2007, I was thinking once more about Sir Edmund. I was facing some difficult circumstances in my life, but I knew, without a doubt, I could climb the mountain standing in my path. I decided to take action after all those years and sent an e-mail to Auckland, New Zealand to an office worker I found who I believed could assist me. I wrote, "If I could have fifteen minutes with Sir Edmund Hillary, I'll get on a plane and fly to Auckland, New Zealand. When fifteen minutes are up, I will return to the United States of America."

The office worker wrote back, "Are you serious about this?"

I replied, "I'm very serious. If can have fifteen minutes of Sir Edmund Hillary's time, I'll fly there, and not surpass my allotted time."

A few days went by and she wrote to give me several different dates that I could consider coming to be with Sir Edmund Hillary in his home. I chose August 31, 2007. When it was only days away, I called a pastor friend of mine from Auckland, Peter Mortlock, to let him know I was soon going to be travelling to Auckland.

"Great, James! What is bringing you to New Zealand?"

"I'm coming to see Sir Edmund Hillary."

"James, you're actually coming to see Sir Edmund Hillary?" Peter questioned.

"Yes, I am. The visit will take place in his home."

"James, are you absolutely sure about that?"

"Absolutely certain," I said.

"You know, James, he is New Zealand's biggest hero. I grew up with the name Sir Edmund Hillary. He's bigger than life down here, Down Under. Are you *sure* you're coming to see him?"

"I'm coming to see him."

"James, this man is on the back of our ten dollar bill."

"I know he's on the back of your ten dollar bill."

"Are you sure you're coming?"

"I'm coming, and I want you and your wife to go with me. We can go together and make a connection to the local church."

I flew into Auckland and Peter picked me up. The next morning, we went over to Sir Edmund Hillary's house at eleven o'clock. We didn't just stay fifteen minutes. They were very gracious and kind and our appointment extended to more than two hours. As someone who values being in the presence of greatness, this was one of the greatest experiences, a highlight, of my life. I was honored to spend time in the presence of a man who had such a great worldview. He was someone who no doubt was reflecting about eternity at the time that I was there.

If you had pulled up into Sir Edmund Hillary's driveway, you would not have known from the outside of that humble home that living behind those walls was one of the great explorers of all time. You would not have guessed that Sir Edmund Hillary and his sweet wife, Lady June, lived there. When we met them, we immediately saw that Sir Edmund was just as unassuming as his house. He was very down-to-earth, humble and a gracious gentleman. He and his wife welcomed us into their home with generous hospitality. It was a warm welcome—a joy and a delight. Most importantly, some of the greatest wisdom that I have ever personally received, I received in those two hours.

I invited five different friends from the United States to go with me prior to calling Peter. None of them took me up on the invitation. Since then, two have come back and said, "If I had it to do over again, James, I would have gone with you for that once-in-a-lifetime visit with Sir Edmund Hillary." Four months and eleven days after our visit, Sir Edmund died. The opportunity was lost.

At some point, each man has to make a decision as to what size of life he will live in our shrinking world. We are each required to decide whether we will live a life beyond the parameters of everyday existence, a life that pursues the largeness of spirit that we see in the life of Sir Edmund Hillary, or if we'll live only to ourselves and our private ambitions.

A man wrapped up in himself makes a very small package.

The first great decision we'll make is to settle the last decision we'll ever need to make and that is the choice of how we will enter the after-life. What do we really believe and are we willing to put it all on the line when the going gets tough?

When I was fourteen years old, I had an experience that left an indelible imprint on my mind. It became a defining moment. I had committed myself to Christ just two years earlier. Now my commitment was going to be tested.

At about ten minutes to two o'clock on a beautiful Friday afternoon, my classmates and I were ready to finish our gymnasium period before the final class at Mary Montgomery High School in Semmes, Alabama. After we finished exercising, we were all sitting on the bleachers in the gym, waiting for the bell to sound.

While I sat, I saw a senior stand and walk to the front of all of the guys in the bleachers. He looked up and asked me to come down to talk to him. I knew this was not going to be a pleasant experience. As I walked down those bleacher steps, I was dreading what might be coming next.

He looked at me, said my name, then, "You're a Christian, right?"

I said, "I am. Christ has come into my heart and life."

He said with sarcasm, "Well, that's great."

Then he snickered and started stirring up the boys to laugh at me. I just stood there, unsure of what to do. He kept goading me.

"Let me ask you a question. If the most beautiful girl at our school wanted to have sex with you, what would you do?"

I could have responded, "I don't want to talk about it," or, "I'm not interested in discussing these things with you." But, I was a new Christian and sensed excitement at the opportunity to share it. I said, "I would not do it. It is not right. It's against the Word of God, and I would not do it."

With my comment, he made sport of me. The other boys laughed. The ring of the class bell seemed like an act of mercy. My discomfort was only to increase. The word got out in the last hour of the day about what I'd said. People spread it further over the weekend. I came back to school on Monday wondering what others may say behind my back and if I'd have to endure the laughs. The incident blew over, but the memory remained.

The boldness I'd shown in that moment, in telling him exactly what I believed, became a defining moment in my life. Any time I was at a place where I needed to make an important decision, the boldness of standing up for what was and is right at age 14, proved to be a lesson that made a difference for a lifetime.

As we embark on this mountain-climbing journey together, we'll be called upon to determine *where* we will live our lives and *how* we will live our lives, at every juncture in the journey.

I think every man is drawn to heroes and I am no exception. As I started writing about that afternoon with Sir Edmund, I reflected on my short tenure of life. I realized that I have always been drawn to people who have a huge spirit or a "spirit of greatness." The spirit of greatness is not revealed in the easy, carefree times of life. Crises will either enlarge and equip us or fill us with fear and faithlessness.

When Christ has come our way, we either shrink and become smaller or we stand and get stronger.

The size we allow our spirits to grow to determines most everything. *We attract who we are, not what we want.*

I've always admired ordinary people who somehow find the conviction, courage, and determination to do extraordinary things. The difference between the ordinary and the extraordinary is the little word "extra." It is the "extra" minutes that make the difference, the "extra" books that prepare the mind, the "extra" exercise that makes one healthier, the "extra" steps taken to go the distance---that moves a person from the ordinary to the extraordinary. The "extra" moves us from being one who simply coasts through life to one who chooses to climb mountains. It is the "extra" that makes someone or something extraordinary.

Have you ever heard that we must walk a second mile to be exceptional? This Everest Life cannot be lived by the first-miler. It is only for the second-miler. The extra mile is the "smile mile." When we look through history we can see where key people went the extra mile and, as a result, changed the course of human history.

A good friend of mine, Dr. Leonard Sweet, wrote an article many years ago about two young men who were in seminary. They were both scheduled to do internships during the summer. The two were walking down the corridor of the seminary, talking about their upcoming internships. Neither of them was happy about where they were going to serve. One student said to the other, "I'm not really excited about where I'm going to do my internship—it just doesn't seem to fit my skills and my abilities."

The other said, "You know, I've been thinking the same thing. I'm not really excited about it, but it is a requirement and I'm just doing it to finish my studies here."

About twenty-five feet behind them, a distinguished professor was walking along. He could hear the conversation between the two Seminarians and started walking a bit faster. When he got close enough to them, he said in a loud voice, "I'm glad that Michelangelo did not say, 'I don't do ceilings.'"

In Dr. Sweet's article, he went on to say that he was glad that Moses did not say, "I don't do wilderness wanderings." Aren't you glad that Daniel did not say, "I don't do lion's dens?" Aren't you glad the three Hebrew children did not say, "we don't do fiery furnaces?" I'm glad Nehemiah did not say, "I don't do walls" and I'm glad Ezra did not say, "I don't do temples." I'm glad David did not say that, "I don't do giants." I'm glad the Apostle Paul did not say, "I don't do persecution and "I don't do letters." Aren't you thankful that Mary, the mother of Jesus, did not say, "I don't do virgin births?" I'm glad that John the Revelator did not say, "I don't do islands and pots of boiling oil." How grateful I am that Jesus Christ didn't say, "I don't do crosses." Aren't you thankful?

Without exception, each of these men and women did the extra. They allowed turmoil and trials to enlarge them rather than discourage them. They chose to stay faithful to the assignment that was before them.

I remember well when I was ten, eleven and twelve years of age being drawn to the front row of the church we attended in Montgomery, Alabama. I just knew that I wanted to be near where the preacher would be. I remember one Christmas my brother and I received matching tape recorders. They were not small ones for children, but large black ones with a handle to carry them and built-in cassette recorders. On one particular occasion, I went to the Pastor Martin and to his wife, Ginger, and requested a particular song I would like the choir to sing. The name of the song was "The King is Coming." I can still hear it in my mind, because I sat on the front row recording it and then played it endlessly until the tape was worn out.

I became a Christian at twelve. As a young teenager, I began fulfilling small leadership positions before larger positions and opportunities presented themselves as I grew. There was always a desire, in my heart, to spend time with the right people in the right place. I wanted to prepare myself, to grow, to mature, to learn and to lead.

In the two hours I spent with Sir Edmund Hillary, I learned more about how to become large enough inside to stand on the roof of my world. The Everest Life is about stepping into a huge environment and learning the insights necessary to grow and become a man fulfilled in his potential and a man who achieves what God desires for him to be.

Half the battle is just in the willingness to show up. *Suit up and show up.* Part of the battle is acquiring the skills that you'll read about in the following pages. Part of the battle is spending time with the right people. Part of the battle is controlling how we spend our lives, our time.

How we use our time determines, to a great extent, the amount of success and fulfillment we will experience in our lives. Others have just as much time as you do and just as much time as I do. It all has to do with how each one makes use of their time. You may have only a minute, but eternity is in it.

Small doors open into big room. We have to stop sizing up the size of the opportunity by the appearance of the door. When we take the small steps God gives us, we will be amazed at what God will entrust to us. An simple example of a small step could be making use of our time reading a beneficial book.

Sometimes, we will have to stoop to walk through small doors. We will never find the room-filled treasure on the other side if we don't stoop to learn, take the first step, or humble ourselves to serve others,.

For each of us, the first door to walk through is to make that first great decision. That is, to accept Christ for who He is, the Son of God, and surrender our lives accordingly. The way we do that is by praying a sincere prayer:

Dear God, I believe in Your Son, Jesus Christ. I want to take this first step, through this small door, to surrender my life to You. I repent of my sin and ask you to be my Savior. Please make me everything that You have created me to become.

As a result of reading this book, you will learn at least four phenomenal answers to four of the most voiced questions every man has to ask at some time in his life. We will also talk about the largest mountain of all. This is a mountain none of us can move on our own. Let's begin this journey to the top of our personal Everest.

Question One
How Can I Become A Focused Man?

How do you get ready for a meeting with one of the greatest men on the planet? If you look at money around the world, you'll see that not too much of it is printed with a living person's face on it unless they are royalty or a dictator. Here I was, getting ready to meet with a man whose face was printed on New Zealand's money. What would I ask him? What knowledge or thoughts did I want to come away with? I pondered this until it was time to fly to Auckland. On the plane, I jotted down what I would ask.

The first question I asked Sir Edmund was simply this: How do I become a focused person?

"There are many adventures in life," I said to him. "There are many things I could be about, many things I can do or try, but how can I become really focused?"

"There are many adventures in life," I commented. "There are many things I could be about, many things I can do or try. But, how can I become truly focuses?"

My wife Sheri and I had buried two babies she gave birth to in the nineteen-nineties. We later adopted two precious daughters from China. Yet, when this trip to Auckland came about, Sheri and I were going through very stressful, challenging days as a result of an attack that occurred in the early years of the Billion Soul Network. Due to where we were in our lives, the question I asked this famous explorer was very fitting. "How can I become focused?"

Sir Edmund sat for a moment. He was very quiet. At the time of our meeting, he was eighty-eight years old. Although he had scaled the heights of his profession, and had experienced much fame and success, he had known his share of sadness as well. He had buried his first wife and their daughter. The pain must have been unbearable. We didn't talk much about those things when we were together. He had lived an enormous life in spite of tragedies he had faced.

Sir Edmund just sat quiet. It appeared that perhaps he had not heard the question. I sat there wondering if I should repeat myself or just let the great man form his answer.

I was happy that I decided to wait for his response. What he said became indelibly imprinted on my mind the moment the words were out of his mouth. In fact, his answer that day became the very essence of what my life's work came to be about with the Billion Soul Network. Sir Edmund said:

"If you only do what others have already done, then you will only feel what others have already felt. But if you would dare to do something that no one else has ever done, then you'll have a satisfaction that no one else has ever felt."

As you ponder the words, they become even more powerful and profound. In every man's life, there is the need for focus and the desire for vision. With vision comes focus. With focus comes exactitude. Exactitude creates priorities for each and every day.

The lack of real, focused vision encourages people to chase aimlessly after *every thing*, trying for the rest of their lives to find that hidden treasure. Once a man has chosen what unique path is his and he knows it is a God-given, divinely-ordained path, he doesn't chase endlessly after doors of opportunities. He knows the path that he is to walk.

I believe that with focused vision also comes the courage that is necessary to fulfill that vision. Edmund Hillary added another sentence after his initial response to the question. He shared:

"When you're choosing your life's project, if there's no fear involved, then you will become bored with it and you won't even finish what you have begun."

After he finished, I asked, "What do you mean by 'fear and boredom'? To me, that's unnatural. I don't want fear but I really don't want boredom."

He continued, "When you are climbing Mt. Everest, there are drop-offs that are two miles down. That fear keeps you from being bored in climbing the mountain."

I wonder if we sometimes choose molehills instead of mountaintops because we don't want the fear of scaling something bigger to gnaw and nag at our lives. As a result, we choose a sub-par life rather than a greater God-filled life.

Once we have settled our first big decision, becoming Christian men, we have to pause long enough to determine what *our* Mount Everest is. Many men think our Mount Everest is working hard enough and earning enough money to retire early and move to a warm place. Maybe some think their Mount Everest is climbing the ladder in a place of employment. No doubt, some men believe their Mount Everest is starting a business and trying to sustain it. I am sure that others see their Mount Everest as trying to climb over health challenges that have come their way or family issues that appear to be insurmountable. Yet, for every Christian man, Mount Everest is not one that we create, not one that we determine to climb, but it is one that has already been decided for us.

As I write today, it's hard to believe, but world population has just crossed seven billion people. The Christian's "Mount Everest" first and foremost is to do the thing Jesus desires for us to do, which is to tell everyone in the entire world about Him. To do so would be the fulfillment of the Great Commission. This fulfillment is the mountain that is unclimbed, the mountain that has never been conquered.

As men, it is okay to set personal goals and try to achieve those goals. There's nothing wrong with setting personal goals and nothing wrong with trying to achieve them.

Yet, the roles and goals that God has for us are bigger than our roles and bigger than our goals.

His goal is that every person on the planet hear the glorious gospel of Jesus Christ. When we evaluate the track record of our Christian faith, we didn't fill the Great Commission when there were only four billion, five billion or six billion people on the planet. Based upon the past, if we continue with our present performance, we will not fulfill the Great Commission while there are seven billion. Likely, you and I will see this population curve cross eight billion and nine billion people.

The Christian's greatest Mount Everest is putting the Cross of Jesus Christ on the roof of the world.

I sometimes wonder how other men measure their lives. As I've meditated on it, I have come to the conclusion that my life is measured on two rails of the same track.

TWO RAILS OF THE SAME TRACK

One side measures Great Commission fulfillment. That side measures my role in helping to fulfill God's goal. It measures my part fulfilling what's in God's heart. When I'm looking at that track, I ask myself, am I making it harder or easier for people to die without ever having received an adequate witness of the Gospel of Jesus Christ? Am I leveraging all that I have to the best of my ability to help finish what is in God's heart, to take the role that God has given me to achieve what is God's goal. Am I abiding by the verse of scripture that says "this ONE thing I do" or am I not focused in what I'm doing with my life?

Am I settling for just one-tenth of the people in the world to know Jesus? Am I settling for just one-tenth of the people in my city or just one-tenth of the people on my street to know Jesus?? Anything less than everyone being reached is not a God-sized goal. God is not interested in just a fraction of the world. He's interested in the whole world. He sent His Son, Jesus Christ, to save the world.

My life is also measured on a second rail of that track. One day I will give an account of my life at the judgment seat of Christ. These two rails on the track of life motivate me. I want the Great Commission fulfilled. I also want to hear the Lord say one day when I see Him, "Well done, thou good and faithful servant." It is the quest to be a better servant of Christ that -becomes the doorway to teachability. With teachability comes wisdom and knowledge.

So, what wisdom and knowledge do we need in order to become that focused man? How about a focused father? Are you, am I a focused leader? No man wants to be a wandering generality. We want to be a definite specific. We want to be men to whom it matters when the alarm clock goes off, because we know what the mission is, what the message is and what the measurement is.

How do we become that focused person? Most have a career, a family, activities and involvements of all kinds. We can have all of that while still keeping our focus on what God wants us to do and be. How do we help put the cross of Christ on the roof of the world?

UNDERSTAND YOUR WORLD

First, if we are going to be measured by our effectiveness to fulfill what is in God's heart, then it is important to understand our world. With the ease of travel and the worldwide access to information through the Internet, it seems plausible that we can finish reaching every person with the Gospel. Take one example:

At the present time, there are approximately sixteen thousand people-groups on the planet. Out of those sixteen thousand people-groups, approximately six thousand of them are considered "unreached," having virtually no witness of Jesus Christ among their populations. The combined population of those unreached people-groups is about 2.4 billion people. Out of those six thousand unreached people-groups, six hundred thirty-nine of them are the largest unreached people-groups in the world, ranging from a hundred thousand in population to many millions. Out of those six hundred and thirty unreached people-groups, three hundred and ten are located in India.

Many men live their lives and never ponder what really matters the most.

A majority of Christians go about their lives working, spending, investing and simply living their lives. How many think about the fact that they will one day give an account of their life, standing before Christ? How sad if they have only the ashes of a wasted life to give to Him. If we fail to place the emphasis where God places His emphasis, then we will miss life's greatest opportunity. We spend so much of our time on "wood, hay, and stubble," things that are *consumed* by fire, rather than "gold, silver, and precious stones," the things that are *refined* by fire.

The Lord desires for us as men to become more than that. He desires for us to have a vision for His world and to do our very best to make it hard for somebody to live on the planet or live in our neighborhood and *not* hear the Gospel.

William Booth was the founder of the Salvation Army. He was one of the greatest visionary leaders of all time and he was persecuted for his faithfulness. He was laughed at and mocked because he chose to work among the poor when many Christians of that day wanted to work among the aristocrats, the wealthy and the affluent. William Booth chose not to do that. When Booth was seventy-five years of age, after staying on his mission for many years, he had an appointment to stand in front of the King of England. The odds had never been in favor of him ever having the opportunity to stand before the King of England. But, after a long, arduous journey, never quitting, never giving in, never giving up, he finally had the opportunity. The king expressed appreciation for William Booth's dedication. When Booth asked to sign the king's book, he took a pen and summed up his life's work with these words:

"Your Majesty," he wrote, "some men's ambition is art, some men's ambition is fame, and some men's ambition is gold. My ambition is the souls of men."

Here's a man who had chosen to become a focused man and put the emphasis where God had put the emphasis. No doubt, when he left this world to meet the King of the Universe, the Lord said, "Well done, thou good and faithful servant."

UNDERSTAND HOW YOU ARE MEASURED

That brings us to the next question, what is the measurement of a real man?

The Apostle Paul was revisiting a strategic mission field, the Bible tells us, and as he came to Miletus, he gathered with him the elders of the Ephesian Church. He took the time to walk and talk with them down memory lane. They talked about the good times they had had together and how God had blessed and poured out His blessings. Paul rehearsed it all. Here is what happened next, starting from Acts 20:36.

"And when he had thus spoken, he kneeled down and prayed with them all. And they all wept sore and fell on Paul's neck and kissed him, sorrowing most of all for the words that he spoke that they should seek his face no more, and they accompanied him to the ship."

Now use your imagination with me. They were one in the bonds of love. They had been through so many prayer meetings and evangelistic crusades together, they'd had so many victories in Christ, that their hearts were melded together. Now, they're having a prayer meeting again on their knees and there is a sweet presence of God's Spirit. And as they're praying, they realize this is the last prayer meeting they'll ever have on Earth with Paul the Apostle.

They began to weep. Not just a few tears, they were convulsing. The Bible says, "they wept sorely." And then they begin to hug Paul. The Bible says they fell on his neck. They're weeping and squeezing him and hugging him because they know they'll never again see Paul. They walked down to the wharf where the ship is as Paul got on the ship. They were parting for a last time.

We are all going to go. All of us are. We may move out of our city, but that's nothing compared to the eternal move we're all going to make. The question we each have to answer is, when we go, what difference will it make? Will your life have had any impact at all?

There is a popular joke about a man who had surgery. He woke up in the recovery room and all the windows were covered with curtains. The blinds were drawn and it was dark. He called to the nurse, "Nurse, open the windows. I want to see outside. Who closed the blinds anyway?"

The question for us is, when we're gone,
will we be missed?

The nurse said, "Calm down, sir, I closed them. There's a big fire across the street and I didn't want you to wake up and think the operation was not a success."

Some of us may not wake up on the other side and see flames, but we may wake up and find our entire lives were not a success. We may find we have wasted our life and are going into eternity with a wasted life. When we go, we will leave behind all that we "have," and take only what we "are." When the world measures a man, they measure him by his brain, his brawn or his bucks. How do you measure your life? How do you think a man is measured?

In the Guinness Book of World Records there's a man named Michael Letito. Do you know what his claim to fame is? He eats glass and metal. He grinds it up and he eats it. That's right. He mixes it with his Wheaties and whatever else he eats. Since 1966, he's eaten ten bicycles, an entire supermarket cart in four and a half days, six chandeliers and a Cessna light aircraft. Now can you imagine this fellow reporting to Christ?

"My son, what did you do when you were on the Earth?"
"Lord, I ate an airplane once."
What a claim to fame. I mean, what really counts? What really matters? Are we going to be focused people? How will we measure life?

OUR MANNER MATTERS

In the twentieth chapter in the book of Acts we see the answer of how a man's life is measured.

First, we learn that the *manner* of a man's life matters. We measure a man by the manner of his life. From Miletus, the Bible says, Paul sent to Ephesus and called the elders of the church. When they came to him, he said, "You know, from the first day that I came to Asia, after what manner I have been with you in all seasons serving the Lord with all humility and mind and with many tears and temptations which befell me by the lying of weight of the Jews" (Acts 20:19).

So, what was the manner of his life? One way we see the manner of Paul's life, is that we see he led a life of *humility*, serving the Lord with all humility.

Nobody has a life that can be called a great life without humility.

There is no true greatness without true humility.

Humility is not putting yourself down. It is not saying you're no good or that not loving yourself is humility. That couldn't be true, because the Bible says that we are to love others *as we love ourselves*. We're to love others as we love ourselves.

What is humility? Humility is an honest estimation of ourselves. It is saying about ourselves what God says about us. The result of humility can be seen primarily in serving.

Notice how Paul said, "serving the Lord with *all* humility." The word "serving" is the verb from which we get the noun, "dulas," which means "bond-slave." Do you know what the mark of humility is? Serving others. A humble person is a person who serves other people. I've often said in our quest to reach one billion people, that if you don't mind being the last zero in the billion, then you can add value to everyone in front of you. It is not the first zero that matters most. It is the last one that adds the most value.

When God measures a man's life, he does not measure that man's life by how many servants a man has, but by how many men the man has served.

There are a lot of men whose lives are going to amount to less than a zero. I'll tell you why. They never learned how to serve. They go to church on Sunday morning and soak it up, but they do not serve. We each need to find a place of service in our church, in our communities, and in our homes. We each need to ask God, "Lord, help me to be a servant." Unless we're truly servants, we will never be truly missed when we're gone.

Not only did Paul live a life of humility, but his manner of life included a life of *heartache*. In that passage of scripture, Paul wrote, "serving the Lord with all humility and all tears." The Apostle Paul had a broken heart. Paul knew how to weep. He knew how to endure the sorrows and hurts of other people. That's the way to be missed. If we live for self and self alone, we will try to insulate ourselves from the cares, toils and problems of the world. When we insulate ourselves from people and their problems, we're not going to be missed. We need to be men who know how to sympathize, men who know how to empathize, and men who have the compassion of the Lord Jesus in our hearts and lives.

Some men don't cry. Perhaps it's been a while since you wept. For many men, we were taught not to cry, not to show emotion. Here is a simple way to learn to weep, even if you've never wept before. Get into prayer and ask Jesus to let you see the world as He sees it. Allow the things that break the heart of Jesus to break your heart.

Shed tears over those you know who have mortgaged their soul to the devil.

Allow yourself to feel the bitter pain of their eternal destiny.

When we read the ministry of the Apostle Paul, we don't often read about him weeping. The only way we know about it in this passage is because he wrote it. He told us. It would appear that most of the time, he wept in private. I can say from my own life that I've shed more tears in my private time than I have in my public time.

"I'm writing out of deep conviction," Paul wrote. Jesus was a man of tears. Paul was a man of tears. Jeremiah was a man of tears. It would behoove us to see their example.

The Apostle Paul said, "I serve the Lord with humility, I serve the Lord with heartache." Then he said, "I've served the Lord with *hardship*."

We learn of some of the trials that befell Paul in the same passage we already read. Paul faced and fought many trials. There were people that disliked him. There were people who were opposed to him. There were men who physically, bodily harmed him because of the stand he took for Jesus Christ. There were people who conspired against him, who were out to get him.

There is no way that we can have a life that counts and make an impression on this world without making some enemies along the way. Unless we're willing to have this manner of life, where we have these three things—humility, heartache, and hardship—we're not going to have the kind of life that Paul had. Without those three, we're not going to have the kind of life that counts.

A man may say, "I don't want that kind of life." Well, maybe he doesn't. Maybe he just wants to be wrapped up in himself, which as was written earlier, makes a pretty small package. But we know that when he's gone, it's not going to make much difference. Nobody in this world will say, "That's the way to have a huge spirit in your life."

OUR MESSAGE MATTERS

Paul had a manner of life and a message in life. Not only do we live a certain way, but we say a certain thing. We're going to leave behind a message. Every one of us will be known for something we've communicated when we're gone. What do you want people to remember about your message? Would they say, "The Gospel of Christ"? That's what I'd like people to say. "This man's life was centered on the message that really matters."

Paul wrote, *"and how I kept back nothing that was profitable unto you, but have taught you and shown you from house to house that is in ever place, testifying both to the Jews and also the Greeks, and that's in every person repentance toward God and faith toward the Lord Jesus Christ"* (Acts 20:20).

The *content* of Paul's message was repentance and faith—repentance toward God and faith in our Lord Jesus Christ. Paul was known primarily as a Gospel preacher. He had a narrow message.

Paul's content had *conviction* in it. *"And now behold I go bound in the Spirit into Jerusalem, not knowing the things that shall befall me, there accept that the Holy Spirit witnesses that in every city saying 'bonds and afflictions abide me'"* (Acts 20:22).

In more modern language, Paul wrote, *"I'm going back to Jerusalem, the Spirit of God wants me to go. I'm bound in the Spirit. That is, I know God's Will for me is to go, and I know that when I get there I'm going to have heartache and trouble."*

Then Paul wrote, *"but none of these things move me"* (Acts 20:24). Another translation interprets it, *"I don't get stampeded by any of these things."*

Paul wrote, *"Neither count I my life dear unto myself so that I might finish my course with joy and the minutes for which I've received the Lord Jesus Christ testify the Gospel, the Grace of God."*

If we want a life that counts, we're going to have to have a message that has the right content and the right conviction.

"I'm bound in the Spirit," Paul wrote. *"None of these things moved me, you're not going to stop me."*

Paul had a bulldog grip on certain things. The average man holds opinions and not convictions. But Paul was a man of deep conviction.

Paul wrote, *"I'm bound in the Spirit, I'm going to finish my course with joy, I will do it. I know what I'm going to do, I will eventually be lead to death."*

We can see from his writing, that Paul would have rather died with a conviction than live with a compromise.

How can we become that focused in our lives? Most of us would far rather live with a compromise than die with a conviction, but we can also understand as we examine his message how Paul became the man that he was.

Paul also had a *confidence* in his message. Paul died with tremendous confidence.

He wrote, *"And now behold, I know that among whom I have gone preaching, the Kingdom of God shall see my face no more. Wherefore I take you to record this day that I am pure from the blood of all men, for I have not shunned to declare to all the council of God"* (Acts 20:25).

In modern language, Paul said, *"You're not going to see me anymore, I'm going to Heaven. But I'm going to tell you one thing, I'm pure from the blood of all men."*

Paul was moved for the souls of men. When he wrote this, he was talking about soul winning. In other words, if we don't tell our friends or neighbors, if we don't tell our brothers and sisters about the Lord Jesus Christ, Paul is inferring that their blood is on our hands.

That is a focused life. Paul made a statement that could only be made by a man who had chosen to stay "on message" until his job was finished. The Apostle Paul knew that before long, he was going to meet the Lord. In view of that, he said, "I am pure. I am free from the blood of all men. I'm not going to face the Lord with bloody hands."

How many men do you know who know their favorite team's statistics, but don't know the names of the lost people that live next door? Do you know a man like that? We have to ask—how is that man going to face the Lord? Will he have blood on his hands?

I can see in my mind's eye the Apostle Paul in prison, tired and aware that his execution is about to come. The burly guard comes toward him.

"Paul, come."

"Where are we going?"

"We're going to the chopping block, Paul. We're going to execute you."

The guard approached Paul with a chain to bind him.

Paul says, "You don't need to put a chain on me. I can walk. It's alright."

So the guard took Paul and they begin to walk down toward the Tiber River, the river that would soon drink the blood of this great man of God. There he goes, the greatest Christian who ever lived. Can you see a hump-backed, older Jewish man, hobbling along, his body bent, broken, and scarred from with the whippings, stonings, and imprisonments.

The guard asked, "Do I hear music? Are you humming?"

"Oh, yes. I didn't know you were listening to me. It's just a song we love to sing—

'It will be worth it all when we see Jesus.'"

The guard snarled, "You're a strange one."

They came down to the river where the executioner was waiting.

The executioner ordered, "Tie him to the chopping block."

Paul quietly said, "You don't need to tie me down. It's alright."

Paul knelt down, putting his head on the chopping block.

They questioned, "Aren't you afraid, Paul?"

"Oh," he said, "I've done this before."

"You can't have done this before!"

"I've died daily," Paul said, with a faraway look in his eyes, knowing the end was here and he would soon see His Savior, the one he had faithfully served.

Paul didn't resist as they put his head on the chopping block. If they asked for his last words, I'm almost certain the Apostle would have said, "Jesus Christ is Lord. Jesus died and rose from the dead for you."

The ax fell falls and Paul was beheaded.

I would like to imagine that the next instant Paul was in heaven, saying to the Lord, " Lord Jesus, you know I wasn't strong, I was not handsome, I didn't have a good voice, I didn't have much money, I didn't have many possessions, but Lord, I kept the faith, I finished my job. Lord, I fought a good fight. My race is over. Lord, these hands are pure from the blood of all men."

What a great way to meet the Lord and enter eternity. I believe in the next instant, Paul would hear, "Well done, thou good and faithful servant. Enter thou into the joy of the Lord. Thank you, Paul, for being true to Me."

We do not want to meet the Lord with bloody hands. Many men may make Heaven, but they will hold in their hands the ashes of a wasted life.

OUR MOTTO MATTERS

How can we be focused in this life? We need to have the right manner and the right message, and the right *motto*. Every man has a motto for his life. Maybe it's put into words and maybe it isn't. There is something that impels him, motivates him, drives him, and constrains him. Paul could say these words:

"I have coveted no man's silver or gold or apparel. You know these hands have ministered unto my necessities and unto them that were with me and I have showed you all things how that so laboring you ought to support the weak, and to remember the words of the Lord Jesus, how he said, 'It is more blessed to give, than to receive.'"(Acts 20:33-34)

Paul had a manner, a message and also a motto. His motto was, "It is more blessed to give than to receive." People can be divided into two categories. There are the takers and there are the givers. The takers eat better, the givers sleep better.

The Apostle Paul was a great man because he spent his life not primarily as a receiver but as a giver. As a result, Paul's life was a blessed life. Scripture teaches us that it is more blessed to give than to receive.

What we have spent is gone forever. What we did not spend is left for others. But *what we give away is ours forever.*

Paul's motto freed him from covetousness. He wrote, "I have coveted no man's silver or gold or apparel" (Acts 20:33).

Paul's motto freed him from laziness. Paul pointed out his work hands and said, *"I have ministered unto my necessities" (Acts 20:34).* He was saying, "I have worked for my needs. Plus, there are people who are weak and there are people who can't work, and there are people who have needs. I work so that I might help the needy." Elsewhere in Scripture we read that if a man won't work, neither should he eat. There are some people who can't work and those of us who can work should work to help those who are weak.

---

*When we die, we're going to take with us
only what we have given away.*

Paul's motto saved him from selfishness. Nobody has a greater life than the man who lives a selfless life. The Apostle Paul lived a life of giving, not taking, of helping, not hurting. His was a life of loving and lifting and caring.

During World War II, the Nazis went into a Polish village and accused all the Jews in that village of crimes against the State. They brought them out of their houses and took them to a field where they were made to dig a ditch that would later become their grave. The Nazis then stripped them of their clothes, lined up the Polish Jews and took machine guns to them. They mowed them down, bullet after bullet flying. The people fell, head over heels into the grave.

A little ten-year-old boy was standing there, naked, with his mother and father. The bullets ripped the parents' bodies open. Blood splattered everywhere. As they fell, the little boy fell with them, but he was not touched by one bullet. He fell into the grave and lay still.

The Nazis saw he was splattered with blood and assumed he was dead like the others. They pushed dirt over these people and the little ten-year-old boy was buried alive. His face was in such a position that he caught a pocket of air. Because the ground was not packed that hard, he could actually breathe while lying on the mutilated bodies of his loved ones. After several hours when it became quiet and dark, he dug his way out of his own grave. He clawed and dug all the way to the surface. This young boy pulled himself out of the mass grave, naked, covered in blood and clotted with dirt.

He went to the house of a neighbor and knocked on the door. The woman who answered the door saw the little boy covered in dirt and blood and the remains of his grave. She recognized him as one of the Jewish boys and knew that he had been marked for death. She screamed at him, "Go away!" and slammed the door in his face.

The little boy dragged himself to another door and knocked. He begged the woman who answered for help but the same thing happened. The woman, in terror, said, "No, I cannot help you, go away."

He went to the third door and knocked on that door and when the woman opened the door, she looked at him and her face froze. Before she could say anything he said to her, "Don't you recognize me? I'm Jesus, that you say you love." She broke and said, "Come in, come in." At the risk of her own life she sheltered that ten-year-old child.

Jesus said, "As much as you have done unto the least of these, my brethren, you have done it unto Me." There is no easy way to have a great life. Millions of men, when they are gone, will not be missed. When other men are gone, people will weep sorely for the loss. These are the men who know the things that count.

The day I asked Sir Edmund how to get focused, he said: *"If you only do what others have already done, then you will only feel what others have already felt. But if you would dare to do something that no one else has ever done, then you'll have a satisfaction that no one else has ever felt."*

We must respond to this challenge by daring to become involved in the Great Commission Christ gave us, to help spread His Gospel down our street, across our city, throughout our nation and into other lands.

Then Sir Edmund further said this: *"When you're choosing your life's project, if there's no fear involved, then you will become bored with it and you won't even finish what you have begun."*

We respond to this challenge by facing the fear of being different from others, by courageously standing up and doing the right thing, by having a proper manner, a good message and by living out our lives according to the right motto.

Here is a prayer you can say right now that could make an eternal difference in your life. How do you measure your life? How have you chosen to walk out the track that God gives you for your life? Are you focused?

Pray this prayer out loud, *"Dear God, right NOW, I want to make the decision to change the way I'm living. Show me how to become involved in the Great Commission right where I am, with my coworkers and neighbors. Show me how to be a help to my pastor. Help me have the courage to stand up and do what You ask me to do after I pray this prayer. I want to get started RIGHT NOW."*

Let's move to the next question I asked Sir Edmund. But first make sure you have these words firmly planted in your mind: If we only do the things that others have already done then we'll only feel what others have already felt, but if we would dare to do something that no one else has ever done then we'll have a satisfaction that no one else has ever had.

Be different. Dare to do what has never been done before in your family, at your work, in your community, church, or in the entire world.

Question Two
What Is Life's Greatest Satisfaction?

No one who ever sets out to find satisfaction is truly satisfied. Satisfaction does not come as a result of personal achievements alone. Real satisfaction is found as much inside as outside and the greatest satisfaction is found as we walk with Christ throughout life's journey, talking with Him, doing what He tells us to do next. On our way to knowing Christ better, we will find the deepest satisfaction in life.

It doesn't take long when you are surfing the Internet or television before you find people who are looking for inner peace, inner joy, and inner satisfaction that will give them a reason for living. It also doesn't take long before you find people who are trying to sell something that promises to satisfy that inner longing.

When I met with Sir Edmund Hillary, I wanted to know what answer he would provide to that deep question. Here was a man who not only was the first to scale the world's tallest mountain. He had also been the first to trek across the continent of Antarctica. Other explorers and adventurers all pointed to the second achievement as being greater, more dangerous, more difficult to accomplish than the first achievement of reaching the top of Mount Everest. He had, in short, done the impossible more than once in his life.

After all the accolades, the achievement, the adventure that he had experienced, which towered over so much of the rest of the world's population, I could not help but to ask Sir Edmund about his greatest satisfaction. Remember that he had already said, "If you do something that no one else has ever done, then you'll have a satisfaction that no one else has ever felt." So, I asked him, "What has been your greatest satisfaction? What has brought more satisfaction to your life than anything else?"

He said, "Well, many people think that the greatest satisfaction in my life is when I climbed Everest. Others think that the greatest satisfaction in my life was the very first time that I crossed Antarctica. Others think the greatest satisfaction of my life was building airports and raising millions of dollars from around the world to help the poor."

These sounded pretty satisfying to me as he slowly ticked off one thing then another, holding out his fingers one by one. Yet, none of these things were his greatest satisfaction.

Finally, he said, "The greatest satisfaction of my life was when I raised enough money to build twenty-seven schools in the Himalaya Mountains for the children that lived there."

He stopped for a moment. Then, with great deliberation, added, "All twenty-seven schools are functioning to this day. The greatest satisfaction of my life was helping young children and young people to learn, to help them equip themselves so they could have a greater and better future."

As he spoke, we were seated in his living room. Later we went outside to his veranda. But from where I was seated right then, just off to one side, I could see his old-style television set with a giant black and white photograph standing on top of it. The picture dominated that part of the room. Nowhere else in any of the areas of the house we entered were there pictures, awards, newspaper clippings, trophies, nothing. There was no trace of the famous picture of Sir Edmund and Tenzing Norgay on top of Mount Everest. There was not even a framed ten-dollar bill.

The picture on the television was a group of about thirty-five young children standing in front of a small schoolhouse. I looked at him, motioned toward the picture, and asked, "Is that the very first school house that you ever started?"

His face broke into a broad smile. "Yes," he said. "The greatest satisfaction of my entire life was when I helped to open the very first school for Himalayan children in the Himalayan Mountains."

Wow, what a statement. Here is Sir Edmund Hillary, one of the most famous men on the planet and he said the greatest satisfaction of his life was not standing on the roof of the world, not crossing Antarctica, not raising millions of dollars to build runways and the other things he did for airports and tourism. The greatest satisfaction of his life was giving to people who could not give back.

The greatest satisfaction of his life was helping others to achieve something they could never achieve by themselves.

It's no different for us right now. To help others achieve in their lives what they would never be able to do by themselves is one of the greatest satisfactions that you and I could ever have. Adding value to others when no return can be added back to us is one of the greatest goals we could have and it will bring the greatest satisfaction. Such a statement is scalable. When you think of the bigger picture, isn't that exactly what Christ did for you and me?

I wonder how many average men could become great men if they viewed their life this way? I wonder how many self-seeking men could become generous men if they measured their life in this fashion? Truly the greatest satisfaction of life is not acquiring things that will soon pass away. The greatest satisfaction of life is investing in others, giving to others, which will never pass away.

Billy Graham said for many years that you never see a U-Haul attached to the hearse on the way to the cemetery. It is a wise man, a wise father, a wise husband who chooses to invest in those things that really do compound in eternal value.

KNOW THE SAVIOR

First and foremost, real satisfaction comes from knowing the Savior. On one particular occasion, at the apex of a celebration, Jesus stood in front of a crowd. He said, "If anyone is thirsty, let him come unto me and drink and he that believes in me as the scripture has said, out of his innermost being shall flow rivers of living water."

Think of it. Jesus said, "If anyone is thirsty..." We need to remember that statement, because *the level of our thirst will determine the level of our satisfaction.* A shallow thirst will provide a shallow satisfaction.

So many Christians spend so much time saying more about more and less about less. They analyze what Jesus said, justify their actions by splitting doctrinal hairs and miss the whole point of what Jesus, the Son of God, actually said. He said, "If anyone is thirsty."

Are we really thirsty? What is the level of thirst? A shallow thirst scans the Internet and television ads and infomercials and buys into shallow solutions. The things of this world provide shallow satisfaction. But a deep thirst for the "extra" in an extraordinary life, for the "more" of life that only Christ can fill will produce a deep satisfaction. Some people say they don't need much, but not because of a deep contentment. It's really because they've allowed their hearts to stay so shallow.

As we realize the secret, we need to *rely on the Savior*. Jesus said, "If anyone is thirsty, let them come." We need to realize the secret is a thirsty heart and the need to rely on the Savior at the same time. He said, "If anyone thirsts, let him come unto *me*." Then He added, "and believe on me, as the scripture has said."

Jesus is holding up a bottomless glass of water and challenges to come and drink what He is offering to us. The deeper the thirst the deeper the satisfaction

---

Imagine for a moment two people walking along in the desert. They come up to a man holding a glass of water. Now, in your imagination, can you see them sitting down with the man and debating about the quality of the water, or where the water came from, or whether it will really satisfy their thirst? Or, can you see them graciously accepting what the man offered?

Jesus was holding up a figurative glass of water. He said, "If anyone is thirsty, let them come unto me." He was creating a word picture to help us understand what He offers us.

The source of satisfaction is Jesus. The force is what He gives. He said, "If anyone comes unto me and believes on me." We believe on Him. Our act of believing is accepting what Jesus Christ has to offer. That is real satisfaction.

We need to realize the secret. Rely on the Savior, and remember His supply. He said, "If anyone is thirsty let him come unto me and drink and he that believes on me, as the scripture has said, out of his innermost being shall flow rivers of living water."

RIVERS OF LIVING WATER

The Apostle John recorded these words of Christ. Both Jesus and John were well aware of the river written about by Ezekiel. Look at what Ezekiel said hundreds of years before Christ:

"The man brought me back to the entrance to the temple, and I saw water coming out from under the threshold of the temple toward the east (for the temple faced east). The water was coming down from under the south side of the temple, south of the altar.

"He then brought me out through the north gate and led me around the outside to the outer gate facing east, and the water was trickling from the south side.

"As the man went eastward with a measuring line in his hand, he measured off a thousand cubits[a] and then led me through water that was ankle-deep.

"He measured off another thousand cubits and led me through water that was knee-deep. He measured off another thousand and led me through water that was up to the waist.

"He measured off another thousand, but now it was a river that I could not cross, because the water had risen and was deep enough to swim in—a river that no one could cross."

He asked me, "Son of man, do you see this?"

Then he led me back to the bank of the river. When I arrived there, I saw a great number of trees on each side of the river.

He said to me, "This water flows toward the eastern region and goes down into the Arabah, where it enters the Dead Sea. When it empties into the sea, the salty water there becomes fresh. Swarms of living creatures will live wherever the river flows. There will be large numbers of fish, because this water flows there and makes the salt water fresh; so where the river flows everything will live.

"Fishermen will stand along the shore; from En Gedi to En Eglaim there will be places for spreading nets. The fish will be of many kinds—like the fish of the Mediterranean Sea.

"But the swamps and marshes will not become fresh; they will be left for salt.

"Fruit trees of all kinds will grow on both banks of the river. Their leaves will not wither, nor will their fruit fail. Every month they will bear fruit, because the water from the sanctuary flows to them. Their fruit will serve for food and their leaves for healing" (Ezekiel 47:1-12 NIV).

Ezekiel wrote about a great and marvelous river, but a *humble* river, a river that flowed underneath the door. It was a humble river, but it was also a holy river, that comes from the Throne of God.

It was a humble river, a holy river, but also a *high-rising* river. Ezekiel wrote, "As the river went, it got wider and it got deeper."

Ezekiel's river was also a *healing* river. As the river flowed through the desert, it brought healing everywhere it flowed, as a result of the fruit trees that were there. The imagery was intended for us to realize that we are to bear fruit in this desperate and dry world. The river brought healing there, but it also brought healing to the Dead Sea. Ezekiel prophesied that one day the Dead Sea would live. We have yet to see that day when the prophecy is fulfilled.

Ezekiel's river was also a *harvesting* river. At the end of it all, not only was there healing in the Dead Sea, but there were fish in the Dead Sea. If you go to the Dead Sea today there's one thing you will not see and that's fish. The second thing you will not see are fishermen. Fishermen and fish go together. Neither are found in the Dead Sea today. But one day, the fishermen are going to catch fish where they never caught fish before. One day, there will be a great harvest at the Dead Sea. When we have the fulfillment of what Christ brings, and we are like a flowing river, it brings a healing and it brings us to live a harvesting life.

Years ago, from one of the greatest Christian men who ever lived, I learned how to bring this river of life down to a real-life experience. In the early 1950's, while Sir Edmund Hillary was climbing Mount Everest, Dr. Bill Bright was starting Campus Crusade for Christ. He was a businessman who had a vision for the world. He said, "I believe that we can touch this world with the Gospel."

Dr. Bright started Campus Crusade for Christ in the 50's, and by the time he graduated for eternity in 2003, what he created had become the strongest Christian ministry in all the world. One day in the late 90's, he and I were having a conversation in his condominium in downtown Orlando, Florida. We were talking about how we measure our life and how we get focused, plus some other related items. He looked at me and said, "What is the greatest privilege in life?"

How many times do we cover up our deficiencies with spirituality?

I said, "The greatest privilege in life is knowing Jesus Christ as my personal savior."

He said that I answered correctly. Then he said, "What is the second-greatest privilege in life?"

Now, I must confess that when he asked that, I did not know how to reply to what was the second-greatest privilege in life. As a Christian, I decided I'd cover up my ignorance with spirituality. I said, "Let me go home and pray about it and come back to you with an answer."

It's sometimes easier to say, "Let's go pray about it," than to do the hard work of solving the problem, thinking through the answer, taking care of the real business at hand.

Dr. Bright smiled and said, "James, we don't need to go and pray about it. You've already, in essence, answered the question. You said the greatest privilege in life is knowing Jesus. Therefore the second-greatest privilege in life is leading someone to the greatest privilege in life.

I was thunderstruck at the simplicity. Dr. Bright had it all figured out. Is it not true? It is not true that the greatest satisfaction in life is knowing Jesus and the second greatest satisfaction in life is leading someone else to Jesus, the first and foremost privilege in life? It's absolutely true.

Dr. Bright was not finished with me yet, though. He looked at me and asked me a question that penetrated my heart. His words will haunt me to the day I leave this earth. He said, "Is your life a reflection of the great two privileges in life?"

Wow! What is the greatest privilege? To know Christ. The second is to lead others to Him. And, because satisfaction is derived as we reach eternal goals, is not the greatest satisfaction found in exercising the greatest privileges?

Dr. Bright in that same conversation said in essence, "Since I came to know Jesus Christ as my personal Savior, as a bond-slave to Jesus Christ, I have measured my life a success if it helped to fulfill the Great Commission. If something in my life did not help to fulfill the Great Commission, I did not write it, I did not speak it, I did not do it, I did not spend it, lest I waste my life on trivial matters."

That was a focused man. That was a man who understood real satisfaction.

DOUBLE BLESSED

Sir Edmund Hillary understood the principle. He understood that we can climb our mountains, we can cross our Antarcticas, but the real satisfaction is not found in personal achievement. The real satisfaction is in helping others, and the greatest help we can provide is in leading somebody to be achievers themselves, leading people to become what they can only become with the assistance of the Lord. The highest point of this is what reaching people for Christ is all about. The highest summit is about leading someone to Jesus Christ when they could not find that salvation on their own. That truly is one of the great satisfactions in all of life.

In Psalms 128, we read these words:

"Blessed is the man who fears the Lord, who walks in His ways, when you shall eat of the fruit of your hands you will be happy and it will be well with you.

"Your wife shall be like a fruitful vine within your house and your children like olive plants around your table.

"Behold for thus shall the man be blessed who fears the Lord.

"The Lord bless you from Zion and may you see the prosperity of Jerusalem all the days of your life; indeed, may you see your children's children. Peace be upon Israel."

Every man wants satisfaction in his home. Every man wants harmony and happiness in his home. Every man wants music and melody in his marriage.

As men, we have to realize that God has called us to be the leader of the band. We set the tone. We set the rhythm. As we lead our band, we determine the harmony, the music, the melody, the symphony of our homes. Real satisfaction is found right here.

It is difficult for us to be good men today. It is even more difficult for us to be good husbands. And more difficult still to be good fathers. I do not have all the answers of parenting, but I do know that you have a God-given authority to practice and to preach and to pray for a family of faith, for raising children with character and for building a legacy that lasts.

The first word of Psalm 128 is "blessed." That word sets the tone for the entire Psalm. "Blessed" means "happy." "Blessed" also means the plural form. What the Psalmist is saying about the person he is describing is clear. He is saying that "happy happy," or "double happy," is the man, the father, the dad who practices certain principles and practices in his life.

Every man wants his family to be a symphony of love for one another, respect for him and praise for God.

On the contrary, if we don't practice what God gives to us, instead of double happiness, we get double trouble. Many families are in failure and many homes are in havoc because they're not living the satisfied life. They're not living the way that Christ has called us to live. One major reason there are so many problems in the home is because so many dads are failing to be the kind of persons and partners and parents that we're supposed to be.

The welfare of the State depends on the welfare of the home. The welfare of the home depends on the spiritual condition of the head of that home. Unspiritual dads will produce unspiritual nations. The safety of the State depends on the sanctity of the home. The sanctity of the home depends on the spirituality of the parents.

THE CHARACTER THAT WE LIVE

How can we have true satisfaction that really matters? First of all, we can have it by *the character that we live.* There's a difference between having character and being a character. We need to make sure that the center of our lives is Jesus Christ. What will our wives remember us for? Will it be for our net worth? Will it be for our leadership skills? Or will it be for our character and our integrity? What will our children remember us for? Will they remember us for our playtime? Yes. Will they remember us for our giving? Yes. Will they remember us being on a cell or computer continually? Yes. But more than anything else they will remember us for our character and our integrity.

Many years ago there was a fine Christian man who was a deacon in his church. He became a pilot in the Vietnam War and was shot down over North Vietnam. His captors told him that he had one hour to live before he would be executed with the other prisoners. He was told he was allowed to write one letter to his family before his death. His wife had died a few months before with cancer; he had only one fifteen-year-old son. His mind raced through so many things he wanted to tell his son. This letter would carry the final words to his son. At first he thought he would write as fast as he could and put down on paper as much as he could. But then he paused and thought, *that's not what I want to write.* He thought for a while longer. *These are the last words that my son will ever read from me.* This is what he wrote:

"Dear son,

"The word is integrity.

"Love, Dad."

When his son received that letter, his dad was already gone, killed in the war. The son read the word, "integrity."

The real word we need to comprehend and apply in every area of our lives, what brings real satisfaction, is the word integrity. It is the character that we live.

THE CONTENTMENT THAT WE LEARN

How can we have true satisfaction that really matters? First is the *character that we live.* Second is the *contentment that we learn.* We read in Psalm 118:2 that as we learn to be content, we find happiness. There is a change in the pronoun from the more general to the more specific in this chapter. We read the words: *when you shall eat of the fruit of your hands you will be happy and it will be well with you.* Notice the words "happy" and "well." They communicate contentment. The picture is of a man who goes out to work, and whether he works from the neck up or the neck down, when he gets home, he's content to live off his earnings in life. He's learned to be content with the things that God gives to him.

The man who loves God the most fears God the most in this life.

As we read through the Psalm, we learn that we are to fear the Lord. *Thus shall the man be blessed who fears the Lord.* The first requisite to be the kind of dad, father and man that God wants us to be is to fear the Lord. The world does not give us that definition. The world does not fear the Lord. The world says that happiness comes from money, material things, fame, fitness, fortune, popularity, achievements and accomplishments. The Bible says, "happy is the man who fears the Lord." The fear of God simply means "love on its knees."

He has a healthy respect for the greatness of God, and a healthy reverence for the goodness of God.

The fear of the Lord is the center of our lives. It is also the circumference of our lives. It provides our lives with proper boundaries. The Word of God, the Lord's Law, has the limits set by God himself. Some things are out of bounds. There are some places we should not go, some books we should not read, some people we should not admire. We must draw the line where God draws the line. We must walk in the ways of God.

THE COMPANION THAT WE LOVE

Thirdly, real satisfaction to a man is coming to understand the value of *the companion whom he loves.*

In this Psalm, the wife is described as a vine: *"Your wife shall be like a fruitful vine within your house.* What does a vine do? A vine grows up a wall, a vine clings to a wall and, as the vine is supported by the wall, the vine is able to grow taller every day. The stronger the vine becomes, the more *fruitful* the vine becomes.

The wife clings to her husband the way a vine clings to the wall. The husband is the strong support to his wife. Just as a vine depends on the support of the wall, so the wife grows and becomes fruitful with the strong support of her husband. The husband is her support and strength. The wife is tender like a vine, is faithful and fruitful in the house. The husband who supports his wife and the wife who clings to her husband will have a happy and satisfied home.

Not only does a vine cling, but a vine climbs. Once a vine has found the support it requires, it becomes his help to develop to maturity. The vine's roots grow down, its branches grow out until it embraces all the space available to accommodate its growth. Given proper protection, given support, given room for growth, the vine will cover the wall. The vine will turn the barest wall into a thing of beauty, covered with wide green leaves and rich purple grapes.

The vine climbs, the vine clings and the vine clusters. It brings forth fruit in abundance. The godly wife is her husband's greatest pride, joy and satisfaction. He's giving her support as she clings to him and needs to be secure. He has given her the room she needs to grow, climbing like a healthy vine.

Now they share the joy of producing a cluster of children to raise for the joy of the Lord. The Psalmist continued, *your wife shall be like a fruitful vine within your house and your children like olive plants around your table.*

THE CHILDREN THAT WE LEAD

The fourth way men find real satisfaction is in *the children that we lead*. The olive in the Bible is the symbol of fruitfulness and righteousness. Our children are like olive trees around our tables. The Psalmist wrote elsewhere, "I am like a green olive tree in the House of God. I trust in the mercy of God forever and ever." The picture he paints is a large green olive tree that has cast its fruit on the ground. Now small olive trees have come from the large olive tree on the ground. The large olive tree has produced itself in the small green olive plants.

Our wives are like vines and our children like olive trees. They are tender and frail. They need to be cared for with tenderness and love. They are not like sticks and stones, but need to be cultivated and nurtured every day.

As men, we tend to blame the problems of the family on anything and everything else. We need to look in the mirror and see ourselves for what we are. Real satisfaction is when our children call us blessed.

The olive is an evergreen. When properly set in the soil, the olive tree displays beauty no matter what the season is. God's goal with our children is to turn them into evergreens, to give them eternal life. That is one of life's greatest satisfactions.

We cannot really teach what we do not know. We cannot come from where we have not been. We cannot give what we do not have. Children are looking to their dads to see an example of integrity. What will children remember about their dads? Their money, their talents, their office, their title? They'll remember his character. You can fool a fool, and you can con a con, but you'll never kid a kid.

The greatest curse on the family is not drug abuse, alcoholism, or generation gap. It is drop-out dads.

A few years ago I heard about a father who was a busy businessman. He was always more interested in making money and writing contracts than investing his time and energy in his family. If you asked him how he would evaluate personal achievement, he would say, "More business, more money, more contracts."

His family was going to move to a new and bigger home. As the man was preparing to leave for work, his wife said, "Now dear, remember, we're moving today, so after work, do not come here, be sure to come to our new home. Don't forget."

"I won't forget."

"I know you," she said. "You're going to forget."

He said, "I won't forget. I'll see you in the new home for dinner tonight."

He worked all day, had contracts to write, phone meetings and business appointments. He worked through lunch and talked on his phone all the way home, preoccupied with his business. He drove to the old address, got out of his car, and started up the steps to his old home, only to realize that all the furniture was gone. The house was empty. Then he remembered that they had moved that day. He said to himself, "Worse than forgetting we moved today, I don't know where we moved to."

As he turned to walk back down the stairs, he saw a small boy on a bicycle looking up at him. He said to the boy, "Do you remember the folks who lived in this house?"

The boy said, "Yes, sir."

"Do you know where they moved to?"

The boy said, "Daddy, Mommy said you wouldn't remember where we moved to, so I'm here to tell you."

A sad joke. Yet, there are still men so preoccupied by their jobs, their money, their success, that they forget what real satisfaction is.

One of the greatest problems today is that it's easy to hire someone else to do our duty, our job. We hire others to do for us what we ought to do. Instead of a dad sitting in his easy chair reading a book to his children, the dad sits his children in front of the television and calls it family time. The dad plugs in a CD or DVD and lets those machines tell his children the stories. Or the dad buys computer software games to entertain the children. When it comes time to teach the child, he sends them off to school and lets the professionals teach them. When it comes time for the child to learn to play sports, he sends them to the professionals. Children need a dad to teach them and lead them. The first word every child learns to spell is love. They spell it: T-I-M-E.

Years ago, just outside Mobile, Alabama, there was a railroad derailment. The train plunged into the swampy water by the track and forty-five people died. I lived in Mobile at the time and one particular news report made a big impact on me. The national news carried a story of a Christian couple that had been on the train. As victims were struggling, trying to get out, this Christian couple saw a young child beginning to drown. Her parents were hemmed in, fastened down by metal that had fallen onto them. There was no way the girl's parents could save their precious daughter, so they were just holding her up, hoping somebody would see her. The Christian couple grabbed the girl, brought her to the surface, and saved her life.

As men, our responsibility is to hold our children up. No doubt most men recognize that the most precious gift God has given us outside of our spouses is our children. One of the greatest satisfactions of life is leading our children to know Jesus Christ as their personal Savior.

One reason we fear the ability to build such a legacy is because of our own backgrounds.

Lastly, real satisfaction to a man is in the contribution that he leaves. The Psalmist talks about the father's grandchildren: *Indeed, may you see your children's children.*

For many of us, one day we will learn how precious our grandchildren are. How tragic for the men who ruin their lives and marriages and never get the satisfaction to know how precious and grand one's "grand"-children are.

Most men fear they are inadequate to build this kind of a legacy. God knows this and He gives us the adequacy. "Except the Lord builds the house, they labor in vain who build it" (Psalm 127:1) We must realize that alone, we cannot build a multi-generational legacy. God has to build it for us.

Some men come from homes where the father was a dropout dad. Others come from homes led by an abuser, or an alcoholic. Some come from homes where they never even knew who their dad was. Because of such upbringings, we can easily excuse ourselves from our duty. We think it won't happen for us. But, we must have the courage to break the cycle, and become the leader of our band.

We cannot do anything about our ancestors, but we can do everything about our descendants. Real satisfaction is the child or grandchild sitting on the knee, loving us and loving Jesus. That is greater than any of the rewards this world could ever promise to give.

Sir Edmund Hillary said we could do something that no one has ever done and have a satisfaction that no one else has ever had. When we choose, as dads, to love our children the way they ought to be loved—perhaps the way we've never been loved—and we bring them up in the saving knowledge of Jesus, we're doing something that no one else has ever done. These are our children, our only children. By leaving a legacy for them, we will have a satisfaction that no one else will ever have.

As the leader of your band, let the music play loud and clear. Find life's real satisfaction not in the things that are passing away, but in what lasts forever.

Question Three
How Can I Overcome Life's Greatest Obstacles?

The foggy morning gave way to a noontime sun, and we shared a cup of tea with Sir Edmund and Lady June. Sir Edmund seemed relaxed, pleased that we were there, and happy to share his stories. His words were slow, measured, thoughtful. I was eager to ask the next question I'd written down during my plane trip down under.

I knew that Sir Edmund had more than one setback in his life. He did not go into much detail on the hard times he'd faced, but I did my research. In 1976, Sir Edmund had raised enough money to fund a second runway to be built for the airport in the Himalaya Mountains. While he'd been lauded by the world for scaling the highest peak, he had reached the summit of Mount Everest with the help of the people who lived at its base. Witnessing the extreme poverty of that population, he had dedicated to use the fame he achieved to help them. He raised great amounts of money for airports in order to promote tourism in the Himalayas. His thought was that increased tourism would increase income in the region, and that would increase the level of living for those very poor people.

Once the second runway of the airport was completed, Sir Edmund invited his wife and sixteen-year-old daughter to take the maiden voyage and fly from that runway back home to Auckland, New Zealand. It was a festive time. People were very excited. Sir Edmund's wife and daughter got on the plane, waved goodbye, the airplane door shut and the pilot moved forward. Sir Edmund watched the plane as it made its way down the runway and took to the skies. As he watched, expecting to see it fade from view, it ascended into the sky and then nosed straight down into a fiery crash. At the end of the runway he had just built, Sir Edmund watched the love of his life, and his oldest daughter be consumed by the fire of the plane crash.

I guessed how he might answer my next question, but I asked it anyway.

"What was one or many of your greatest obstacles in life?" I said.

Sir Edmund said his greatest obstacle in life was not overcoming Mount Everest or climbing Antarctica or any of the other projects he took on. He said the greatest obstacle he faced was the loss of his wife and daughter. He went on to say that in general, life's greatest obstacles and problems are not those on the outside but those on the inside.

Life's greatest obstacles and problems are not those on the outside but those on the inside. Haven't you found that to be so true in life? I have.

Sir Edmund went on to say that it took him several years to overcome the grief and sorrow of that fatal accident. Even though it was not his responsibility, he took responsibility because he encouraged his loved ones to take the flight that would ultimately take their lives. Even though everything he had done was safe and did not contribute to the wreck, it took him several years to overcome the tragedy, understandably.

During that deep dark time in his life, he turned to alcohol and other things to cope with what seemed like insurmountable grief that he was facing. He walked up and down that runway weeping. He looked at the mountains in the distance as he cried out his sorrow. He was upset with God Himself because in his mind God had allowed his wife and daughter to be taken away.

No wonder he could say that the biggest mountain that a man will ever face in his life is not the mountain he chooses to physically climb, but the mountain that no one else sees inside. Those emotional mountains he said became some of the hardest mountains he would ever climb in his life.

Sooner or later each man will face daunting and dark times. My wife and I have. We have walked a Trail of Tears on different occasions with the passing of our children many years ago and other sorrows. No matter who you are, you can't escape it. One day, sickness will come. One day, sadness will be knocking on your door. One day, grievous situations will come to you and me. It's just a matter of time. We get sick, we get better. We get sick, we get better. But in this life, one day we will get sick and we won't get better.

There comes a time when death comes for you. It will come for me. It comes for the rich. It comes for the poor. Regardless of who we are, we can't escape it. So sooner or later, we will walk through a terrible and sad time. Without Jesus Christ, we are hopeless—without hope. But *with* Christ we have the "blessed hope." That's not the "blessed escape," but the blessed *hope* that one day we will leave this world, forever to be in the presence of the King of the Universe.

There is a familiar passage of Scripture that most Christians know, from John's Gospel. It's where John records the time when Jesus walked on the water. Read the account:

"Jesus therefore perceiving that they were intended to come and take him by force to make him King, withdrew again to the mountain by himself alone.

"And now when evening came his disciples went down to the sea and after getting into a boat they started to cross the sea to Capernaum.

"And it had already become dark and Jesus had not yet come to them. And they began to be stirred up because a strong wind was blowing.

"And when, therefore, they had rowed about three or four miles, they beheld Jesus walking on the sea and drawing near to the boat and they were frightened, but he said to them, 'It is I, do not be afraid.'

"They were willing therefore to receive him into the boat and immediately the boat was at the land to which they were going" (John 6:15).

From this passage, we can learn numerous steps we can take to overcome life's greatest obstacles. I don't know how people believe they can achieve it by themselves. As believers and Christ followers, as Godly men, we *can* overcome life's greatest problems and obstacles.

GOVERNED BY GOD'S PROVIDENCE

First, *we are governed by God's providence.* Jesus encouraged the disciples to get into a boat to go to the other side of the lake. But, He already knew they would face the storm of their life before they reached the other side.

We need to realize as men that we are governed by God's providence.

We see the word "providence" sometimes, but what does that word really mean? The word "providence" comes from the Latin word "vida" from which we get the English word "video," which means "to see." Put "pro" in front of it, "provida," "provideo," or "to see ahead of." Providence literally means "to see ahead of time."

God sees ahead of time. He saw me before I started writing this book. He saw me before I finished it. He saw you before you acquired it. He saw the two of us ahead of time.

Jesus knew. He knew that the disciples, when they got into the boat to cross the Sea of Galilee, were going to be in the greatest storm of their lives.

Every day the Lord orders our steps and our stops.
There is not a thing that catches the
Holy Trinity by surprise.

When storms come our way, when death knocks on our door, when tragedy strikes in our home, we can feel that we're all alone. We think God didn't see it, and no one cared. The truth is, not only are you not alone, but the Lord saw it before it ever happened. Not only did He see it, but God made a way to take care of us long before the tragedy came our way.

There's not a thing that happens that God does not know about ahead of time. It has been said that the safest place to be is "in the will of God." That means, doing God's will, what He wants us to do. I'd rather be walking at half-past midnight in the scariest city in the world *in* God's will, than out of God's will sitting in my easy chair at home. This doesn't mean that being in God's will is bliss and blessed ever minute. It doesn't mean everything is happy and exciting. But in God's will, we get God's way. And with God's way, we get God's victory.

If you're facing a heart-wrenching disaster in your life right now but you're in fellowship with Christ, then the Lord is not against you. He is for you. When you submit it to Him, in the process of time, He will turn these things around for your good and for God's glory.

GROWING BY GOD'S PLAN

We are governed by God's providence, and secondly, *we are growing by God's plan.* This is a tough step to accept when we're walking through a deep, dark time in life. The truth is, we grow more in a time of storm than in a time of peace. We grow more in a time of hardship than in a time of easiness. Faith is like film—it is best developed in the dark.

Let's be honest with ourselves—when do we grow the most? When do we pray the most? When do we study God's Word the most? When do we spend time with the right people the most? When do we eliminate the negative factors in our life the most? It is when we're walking through the most difficult times in our life.

God desires for his disciples to grow. He does not want us to stay where we are. A year from now, I encourage you not be to praying the prayers you're praying now, living the life that you're living now. Decide that you're going to live in the apex of the leadership triangle, in the top five percent of men who see the sun come up sooner than others do and see it stay up longer than the other men do. It is in that area of life that God has called us to live our life.

We're going to be bigger and better people. We're going to have a larger spirit and a bigger heart.

Things that used to frustrate us won't frustrate us because we outgrew them.

Things that used to matter to us won't matter to us because we got bigger and larger and more focused. We won't be as interested in stance as we are in souls. We won't be as interested in games as we are in the Gospel. We won't be as interested in the things that pass away as we are in the things that are eternal, because we're growing by God's Plan.

We made a decision to read through the Bible each and every year. We made a decision to spend time with the right people. We made a decision to become the man that God desires us to become.

Christ's disciples would never be the same. They came to understand that the Christ on the seashore was also the Christ of the storm. *The Christ that ordered them to get in the boat was the one that was going to take them through to the other side.*

GRACED BY GOD'S PRAYERS

As I've traveled over the last three decades, from time to time people come up to me and say, "I just want you to know, I'm praying for you." Every so often I get a text or an e-mail that says, "I'm praying for you." When I see that someone is praying for me, it moves me. To know that I was important enough to a person that they would call my name out in prayer; that I was on the mind of somebody's life to the point that they would intercede for me in prayer means so much. There are some things we can get in life. We can get more groceries. We can get more gasoline. We can get more of many things in this world. There is one thing we cannot get, and that's more time. We either use time or we lose it. When someone tells me that they're praying for me, they're not only giving me their prayers, they're giving me their very essence, their time. That is beyond comprehension.

So how do we climb up and over our obstacles? We do it by realizing that we're governed by God's providence, growing by God's plan, graced by God's prayers.

What did the Lord do? The Lord encouraged those early disciples to get into that boat and cross to the other side, but He went up to the mountaintop alone to pray, as was His custom. We know that he went there to pray.

What's interesting about the story, is that within three to four miles, those early disciples were in the storm of their lives. They were looking around. They could not find Jesus. That is the impression of this story. They were looking, but they couldn't find him.

Fear gripped their hearts and lives. The storm was roaring and beating against that small craft. Jesus was alone, praying. Even though they couldn't see Jesus, Jesus could see them. Even when we can't see the Lord, the Lord can see us. And the Bible says that we're on the prayer list of the King of the Universe. The Bible says that Jesus is praying for us. In fact, He is "making intercession for us" (Hebrews 4). Jesus prays for the people of this world. He especially prays for those who are His followers. And, sir, I want you to know that Christ is praying for you.

How do we overcome life's greatest obstacles? Not just because we're strong enough, not just because we're smart enough, but because Christ is praying for us.

Christ is praying that we will overcome, that we won't falter and fail, that we won't quit and give in but we'll rise to the challenge, that we'll rise above it and be victorious. It is one thing for a man or woman to pray for you and me, it is one thing for a loved one to pray for you or my loved one to pray for me, but we're on the prayer list of the King of the Universe. Jesus Christ is praying for us.

Now think of this. How many prayers do you think He has prayed that the Father has not heard? How many prayers do you think He has prayed that didn't get to the Father? How many prayers do you think He has prayed that have not been answered? We all know the answer.

Every prayer that He's prayed, God the Father has heard. Every prayer that He has prayed has reached the Father. Every prayer that He has prayed has been answered by the Lord Himself.

Christ is praying for you and He's praying for me. I have known without a doubt from time to time that it has been the prayers of God's people and the prayers of Christ Himself that have given me the strength to keep on keeping on when every nerve and fiber in my body was screeching and crying out for me to quit or give in.

GUARDED BY GOD'S POWER

How do we overcome life's greatest obstacles? There is nothing that comes to you or to me without God's divine permission. There is not a storm that hits us, not a wind of worry that comes our way that Christ does not permit to come our way. We are guarded by His power.

It is interesting to me that even though those disciples in the storm were full of fear and completely afraid, there was really no reason for them to be afraid and there was no reason for them to worry. Over the years, I've traveled a lot by airplane. The thing about airplanes is that you want your landings to equal your take-offs. If you land as many times as you take off, you're going to be okay. I've been on some flights that felt they like would be the very last flight I was going to take.

I was on a particular flight on one occasion when an engine went out. There were only two engines to start with, so we made an emergency landing. I was on another flight where the wheels struggled to descend on the airplane. The struggling wheels shook the plane and shook the plane until they finally came down and we landed in Chicago. I remember one time my wife and I were on a plane and we were so exhausted that we went to sleep right away. We were soon awakened to learn that the hydraulic system on the airplane was not working well. The pilot came on the intercom and said, "You can expect to see ambulances and fire trucks, but do not be alarmed." Telling us that everybody else is so concerned that they're going to bring out the fire trucks and the ambulances is not reassuring when he ends by saying we shouldn't be afraid! His comments had the exact opposite effect.

There have been times in my life where I wondered, "Am I going to see the sun rise again? Am I going to make it through this ordeal?" And I've come to realize over the years that we are truly guarded by His person, guarded by His power and that He does protect us, He does preserve us. There are times when we don't even realize it that He's looking out for us. There are times when we don't even realize that He's going out of His way to make sure we're safe and secure.

If you're struggling with a great challenge that has come your way, when the heartache and tears seem that they will not stop flowing, remember that God is for you and not against you.

He is going to work it out for your good. Somehow, some way, you will look back and say, "In the midst of it all, He was protecting me. In the midst of it all, He was guarding me. He was keeping me safe and secure."

These disciples on that boat saw those waves that were bigger than the boat. They saw the water getting in the boat. No doubt they were thinking, "This is the last boat ride we're going to be on, we're not going to make it to the other side."

HOW CAN I OVERCOME LIFE'S GREATEST OBSTACLES?

But the Lord was teaching them that "Where I send you, I take care of you. Where I send you, I will make sure that you're going to be alright."

GLADDENED BY HIS PRESENCE

And how do we overcome life's greatest obstacles that come our way? We practice living in the presence of the Lord. When we practice living in God's presence, He gives us the ability to overcome life's greatest challenges.

Jesus is always with us. When those disciples were out in the middle of the storm, with Jesus gone from them, out of sight, in reality, Jesus was coming down from the mountainside to the seashore. Jesus calmly walked right out onto the ocean. He walked several miles across the windswept waters to where they were.

They looked up and finally saw Jesus, walking on the water. And when Christ came to them, He said "It is I, be not afraid."

Note that He said, "I am." This is the same phrase that Jehovah said to Moses at the burning bush.

Moses said, "Who are you?"

God said, "I am that I am."

In other words, God was saying to Moses, "I will be what you need me to be while you're in Egypt. I will be what you need me to be when you're in front of the Pharaoh. I will be who you need me to be when you lead the nation of Israel."

Christ came across that stormy water and said, "I am." When He said that, He was saying, "I am who I am. I am the God of Abraham, Isaac, and Jacob. I am the God of the Old Testament and the New Testament. I am the creator of all things between heavens and earth. I am who I say I am. I will be what you need me to be. I will be the one who takes care of you in the midst of the darkest storm."

Jesus was walking across that water to those disciples. As He walked, what was under His feet was over their heads. Those waves were pounding across the top of that boat. The waves were bigger than them. They were afraid that this was the end for them. Instead of going over, they were going to go under.

The first thing Jesus said was, "I am." The second thing He said was, "Be not afraid." That passage always brings a smile to my face when I read through it. Jesus is telling them not to be afraid, and yet they're in a fearful place. Scared to death. Certain death is coming.

Moses said the same thing to the nation of Israel when they were staring at the Red Sea. He said, "Stand still." And then he said, "Be not afraid." God had brought them to a fearful place and then He told them not to be afraid. Jesus brought the disciples to a fearful place and then told them not to be afraid.

If you are in the midst of a fearful place in your life, I want to encourage you not to be afraid. One of the ways you can do that is spend time with Jesus and spend time with His Disciples. Spend time with fellow Christ followers. Unpack your thoughts with friends and encourage them to pray for you.

What was under Jesus' feet was over their heads. That means today, whatever is over your head is still under His feet. When what is over your head is under His feet, you're going to make it to the other side. You may not know how. You may not know when. But, you're going to make it to the other side. The new day will come. The grief will be gone. The tears won't flow as much as before and you will have reached the other side.

It is God's Presence that gladdens us. It is God's Presence that give us hope and comfort. It is God's Presence that lets us know everything is not bleak and bad. He's going to help us get to the other side.

When my wife and I lost our two children in the 1990's, I came to understand that a cliché never heals a broken heart. When I walked through a deep dark time in my personal leadership life when an attack came to my life's work, I came to understand that simple words alone never heal a broken heart.

Maybe you are walking through grief. Maybe the sun has set and you're wondering when the sun will rise again. You may wonder, *How can I overcome life's greatest problems? How can I be the dad or the husband that I need to be to show my family how to overcome when life seems overwhelming?*

Jesus Christ comes walking on the water. And as He comes walking across the water, He says, "I am." He says, "Be not afraid."

GUIDED BY HIS PURPOSE

What happens next in this story is one of the most amazing passages to me in all of the Bible. Jesus got in that boat and immediately they were on the other side. When they got to the other side, they met a demoniac. This may sound like they went from a bad situation to a worse one. But it wasn't so. Jesus calmed the storm at sea, and then he calmed the storm raging in that young demoniac's life. He set the man free. From that day forward, that man became one of the great young evangelists of that day, heralding the Gospel to his community, telling them about Jesus.

What was Christ's real purpose? His purpose was to get to the other side. On the other side was another man who needed to come to the saving knowledge of Jesus Christ.

What is our purpose in this life? Our purpose in this life is to follow in the footsteps of Jesus Christ, our Lord and Savior. He gets us from one side to the other side. He gets in the boat of our lives and helps us to cross the sea of time, from earth to eternity.

The purpose is to get from here to there, to get from earth to heaven. That is the purpose. Through the ebb and flow of life, through the happy times and the hard times, through the joy, sickness and sadness, the boat is still on course. The boat is going to take us to the other side.

The Bible says Jesus got into that boat and immediately they were to the other side. When Jesus stepped into that water, He was overcoming gravity. But when Jesus stepped into that boat and it was taken immediately to the other side, He overcame time.

One day the Lord Jesus Christ is going to step out of the portals of glory. He is going to come down through the starry spangled skies of Heaven. He's going to walk out onto the clouds of time and He's going to be making walking on the water look like child's play. On that day, He'll be walking on the clouds, with the diadems of heaven on His head and a rainbow of victory wrapped around His shoulders.

One day Jesus is going to step into our lives and immediately and instantly we're going to be standing on the other side.

We will be standing on the side called heaven on the seashores of eternity. We will look back across the seas of our life and our time upon this earth and we'll realize that *the Lord Jesus Christ never promised us smooth sailing but He did promise us a safe landing.*

Jesus never said it wouldn't be rough and tough. He never said it wouldn't be challenging and hard, but He did say we're going to the other side. That means, regardless of what life throws at you, regardless of how difficult it may be, regardless of how much pain may come your way, you're going to the other side. There are not enough devils in hell, there are not enough demonic spirits on earth, there are not enough mean people upon this planet that could stop you from going to the other side. One day you will stand upon the seashores of heaven and you'll realize that throughout life's journey, through the ebb and flow of life, whether it be walking across the narrow things or climbing the tall things, God was taking care of us. He was leading us one step at a time.

Sir Edmund said that life's greatest obstacles and problems are not those on the outside but those on the inside. The faith to know that Jesus is right here with us is what overcomes that obstacle for us. The Lord Jesus Christ makes us victorious in our homes, in our jobs, in our life now and forever, as He keeps under His feet what is over our heads, and takes us to the other side.

Question Four
When Should I Get Started?

Sir Edmund continued speaking for a while after he gave that first great answer: "If we only do what others have done, we'll only feel what others have felt." But then he added another important sentence. It was about taking action. Sir Edmund said, "Once you've decided what it is you're going to do, start right now." From there, he said a whole lot more.

We talked for a bit about procrastination. I shared my belief that the sin of procrastination has damned more souls to hell than any other sin. It is generally thought of as a benign little sin. Yet, it has likely caused the greatest failures in people who could have achieved a great, divine destiny. Sir Edmund was nodding in agreement.

"Once you've decided what it is you're going to do, get started," he said. "I'm eighty-eight years old now and there are six projects I will never be able to do."

When he gave the precise number of projects, I was thinking about perhaps another school built, or a book written. Maybe he needed to clean out his garage. Maybe he needed to take care of some personal matters. Curiosity bit at me, so I asked him, "Would you mind telling me at least one of those things that you will not be able to do?"

He sat quiet for a moment then said, "I'll be glad to tell you one of them." Pause. "In 1955, I was the very first one to cross Antarctica."

My thought process pretty much blew up right then. I was thinking about a book project or some personal items. He was thinking about a landmass. He was thinking about a continent. When you're in the presence of greatness, just being there and catching a glimpse of how that man thinks can be life-expanding.

Sir Edmund said, "James, you know, some say crossing Antarctica was harder than climbing Mt. Everest."

I am not really able to judge which is harder. I have never done either. I have never considered either one. I especially would not have considered either one if they had never been done before. Such thoughts never occurred to me. But that is how Sir Edmund's mind operated.

He went on to say in essence that he was at the bottom of the earth, crossing Antarctica, and came to a mountain range. He climbed to the top of that mountain range, looked across the glacier and saw animal life and sea life. He thought, *I will climb down this mountain, crawl across the ice of that glacier. I'll get on the other side. I'll climb the other mountain range and look at the view from there.*

But then another thought took hold of him. *No, no, no, no, no, that's not necessary, I'm still a young man, I'll come back another day, and I will climb down that mountain, I will cross that glacier, I'll climb the other mountain.*

He said that now he was eighty-eight years old. The years came and went and he never got back to that glacier in Antarctica. He was never able to climb that mountain. He was never able to cross that glacier. He was never able to climb the mountain on the other side and he knew he never would since, as he said, "I'm too old now."

Well, this is useful information, historical, and helps us get a sense that life is short and whatever we're going to do, we should get after it. But he didn't just stop with that. Choosing careful words, he then said:

"In every man's life there are two seasons. There is a season when time and energy work against us, and there's a season in our life when time and energy work for us. But we never know what season we're in until we attempt a project bigger than we are."

That just hits at the core of the issue right there. What a wise lesson. We as men have only two seasons in life. One when time and energy work for us. One when time and energy work against us. But we'll never know what season we're in until we try to do something that is bigger than we are.

Then he punctuated his statement again with this: "So therefore, whatever you're going to do, do it right now."

We went out on the veranda and saw the sweeping view of the countryside afforded by his lovely home. We ended our time together with prayer, then he signed three books for me. I probably have in my library the last books that Sir Edmund Hillary ever personally signed. He signed one for my oldest daughter Olivia, one for a friend who one day I will give a book to, and one for me personally. I noticed that as he was signing my book, his hand was shaking. The book was shaking as well. Time and energy were working against Sir Edmund Hillary so much so that signing a book was difficult. Yet, there had been a time when those same hands could climb a mountain. Those same hands could cross Antarctica. Now, it was hard for those hands to autograph a book.

It is up to you and me to make sure that we have enough time, energy, and discipline to fulfill our divine destiny.

So many men waste their time, waste their energy, and then late in life they try to take on the big stuff only to fail, because they allowed the window of time to close on their dreams. They thought they still had time when, in fact, they did not have the time. They thought they had enough energy when, in fact, they did not have enough energy.

Whatever we're going to do, we need to do it now. Whatever we're going to be as men, we need to become that now. We have to become the man that Christ desires for us to be, become the dad that God ordained us to be, become the leader that only we can become in this life. We have to do it before it is eternally too late.

For every man, and energy will work for us and finally, time and energy will work against us.

I think about Caleb, one of the great, great leaders of the Old Testament who lived his life in wilderness wanderings for forty years. But on his eighty-fifth birthday, as he was about to finally enter into Canaan, he said in essence, "I want this mountain. I want to stand on the top of my world in the way that I have in my heart. I want to hold it in my hands."

The largest projects ahead of us are the ones that we are to tackle right away, because one day, time and energy will work against us just as much as time and energy today are working for us.

What are some practical ways in which we can get in motion, get in synch, with what is important so we don't look back on wasted dreams and wasted destinies? Let's look to Caleb for answers, that great conqueror from a distant, bygone era. Watching his life helps us to know how to be one who is achieving what really matters in the time that the Lord has given us upon this earth. Learning from him will help us to get out of the gate, to get started and to be faithful all the days of our lives. This is part of his story:

"When they had gone up into the Negev, they came to Hebron where Ahiman, Sheshai and Talmai, the descendants of Anak were. (Now Hebron was built seven years before Zoan in Egypt.) . . .

"When they returned from spying out the land, at the end of forty days, ²⁶they proceeded to come to Moses and Aaron and to all the congregation of the sons of Israel in the wilderness of Paran, at Kadesh; and they brought back word to them and to all the congregation and showed them the fruit of the land.

"Thus they told him, and said, "We went in to the land where you sent us; and it certainly does flow with milk and honey, and this is its fruit. ²⁸Nevertheless, the people who live in the land are strong, and the cities are fortified and very large; and moreover, we saw the descendants of Anak there. Amalek is living in the land of the Negev and the Hittites and the Jebusites and the Amorites are living in the hill country, and the Canaanites are living by the sea and by the side of the Jordan."

Then Caleb quieted the people before Moses, and said, "We should by all means go up and take possession of it, for we shall surely over come it."

But the men who had gone up with him said, "We are not able to go up against the people, for they are too strong for us."

So they gave out to the sons of Israel a bad report of the land which they had spied out, saying, "The land through which we have gone, in spying it out, is a land that devours its inhabitants; and all the people whom we saw in it are men of great size.

There also we saw the Nephilim (the sons of Anak are a part of the Nephilim); and we became like grasshoppers in our own sight, and so we were in their sight (Numbers 13:22, 25-33).

I have personally enjoyed following the Lord because that is where the faith, the fight and the victory are. There is no victory without a battle. God has called His people to live on the mountaintop and to experience the blessings, possessions and purposes of His design. When you are a believer and follower of the Lord, He has bigger and brighter things in store for you than you have ever imagined.

In this passage, God had brought His people to Kadesh-Barnea. Moses sent twelve spies into the Promised Land for forty days. When they returned, ten bore a negative report. Only two were positive about God's plan for possessing their new land. The people chose to believe the negative reports. Only Joshua and Caleb believed the Israelites could possess the land and do what God had called them to do.

What made Caleb different from ten of the other eleven spies? What caused Caleb to have victory in his heart and believe the Israelites could possess their possessions and fulfill what God had planned for them?

Before we have a mountain in our hands, we must first have it in our hearts. We will never possess it physically until we possess it spiritually. Many of God's people are living in a wilderness inside, instead of a mountain. God wants each of us to have a mountain in our hearts and know how to make it happen.

WE MUST SURVEY OUR CHALLENGES

The first step in having a mountain in our hearts is to survey our challenges. Israel was facing a lot of challenges. Jesus talked about "counting the cost." Before we launch out, we must count the cost, understanding what it will take, so we will be willing to pay the price. We need to survey our challenges. Israel's challenges were fourfold.

The enemy was strong in pride. Three names were mentioned at the start of this story. The Word of God lists these three names for a reason. The meanings of these names are important. Ahiman means "what I am," Sheshai is translated "who I am," and Talmai means "what I can do." Nephilim was saying to the Israelites, "Come over here and we will show you that you cannot defeat us." They knew they were a strong and gifted people. They were strong in pride. The battle to which we are called is one of difficulty.

There are people in the world you will encounter who have tremendous pride in who they are and what they can accomplish.

Understand it. When you are facing an enemy of the Cross, that enemy is going to be strong in pride.

The enemy was strong in position. The Bible says Nephilim had walled cities located on mountaintops. They had a very advantageous position of strength. They were saying to the nation of Israel, "We have leverage over you." Today there are people in high positions who do not want the Bible or a spiritual awakening. When you encounter them, remember that nothing is too difficult for Almighty God.

The enemy was strong in population. The adversary was strong in pride, in position and in population. We read in the Bible that they "devoured the land." They were so numerous they filled the land. They had an overpopulation problem that was devouring the land. That's how numerous they were. Even today, more people do not believe in Jesus than those who do. There are more in Satan's kingdom than those who are in God's. This is the very reason that the battle for souls is the greatest battle of life. We have to overcome the obstacles of the enemy and win people to Christ.

The enemy was strong in proportion. These were giants who were eight and nine feet tall. They were part of the Anakim, a race of giants. The Hebrew people were small in comparison. You may be up against problems of gigantic proportions, just as Sir Edmund was when he faced Mount Everest. Remember that it does not matter how large the crowd, where they are, or even who they are. The fact is that God plus one—anyone—always equals a majority. God is calling us to a fresh challenge to see the land, possess it and go where He wants us to go.

As we survey the challenges, ones that look more confident and plentiful, stronger and bigger, we must keep our attitudes positive before God and others. Whatever is happening around us, we can always choose to have the right attitude. Some people seem to be mostly optimistic while others appear to be mostly pessimistic. What kind of attitude do you have?

I heard a story about the parents of nine-year-old twins. One twin was very optimistic about most things that happened in life while the other was very negative. Naturally, these parents were concerned and turned to a psychologist who suggested the parents try to balance the children's personalities. For Christmas they should give the best gifts to the negative child and the not-so-nice gifts to the positive one. He also suggested they go to the extreme and give a box of manure to the positive twin.

On Christmas morning, the parents watched each child open his gifts. Sure enough, the negative child complained about the kinds and colors of his gifts and that his friends already had better gifts than these.

The positive child ripped into his box of manure, and started plowing into it with his hands. He was laughing. It seemed he was thrilled with the manure. The parents asked him why he was so happy with his gift. He said, "With this much manure, I am sure there is a pony in here somewhere."

As we survey the challenges of the enemy, we must remember our attitude will make a difference. Try to see the challenges as bridges that will enable us to accomplish things for God. Not only do we need to survey the challenges while keeping a good attitude, we also need to stimulate our courage.

WE NEED TO STIMULATE OUR COURAGE

Courage is required for overcoming the challenges. Caleb had courage. Our prayer should be, "Lord, give us the courage of Caleb—courage to believe we can possess our possessions, conquer our Canaan, and enter into what God has for us."

How do we stimulate courage? Courage is stimulated by using the Word of God.

We must look at it from God's perspective. When Caleb brought the good report to the Israelites, they couldn't believe it. The Israelites were not looking at how big God was compared to the giants. Instead, they kept expressing how small *they* were compared to the giants. They said they were "grasshoppers" by comparison. Israel had a "grasshopper complex." The grasshopper complex is always looking to see how large everything is. This complex did not allow them to look down on things. They had a complex and did not see things as God saw them.

"We are seated together in heavenly places in Christ Jesus" (Ephesians 2:6). If we are seated together in heavenly places with Christ Jesus, then we can look down on things rather than look up at them. We can have the perspective God wants us to have.

Too often our outlook is negative. All we see are the giants of doubt, disappointment and disease. We see the giants of depression, financial crisis and broken homes. We see the crisis on the job or at school. When our eyes are not on the Lord, it is easy to perceive the giants. We just have to take our eyes off the giants and believe God can lead us into victory.

Because the people of Israel did not see things from God's perspective, they all died in the wilderness except for Joshua and Caleb. It is possible you may think your problems are too big. If so, you will miss the victory and die in the wilderness. I have seen some Christians resist God moving on their behalf, as He did for the Israelites, and dig in their heels as if to say they do not want what God wants to do. God looks for those who are willing to trust and follow His leading.

Even though Caleb was in the wilderness, he had a mountain in his heart. He had seen the land flowing with milk and honey. He had seen the mountains and the beauty of the land. He kept that mountain in his heart.

You may be living in the wilderness and there may be difficulties and problems in your life, but there can be a mountain in your heart.

See what God can do with a people who are willing to go with the Lord. Caleb had God's perspective and so he made it to victory. Learn to have the heavenly perspective about everything in life.

Some time ago, a lady was taking her first flight on an airplane. Shortly after taking a seat by the window, she began to say, "It's true! It's true! It's true!" She closed her eyes and continued, "I can't believe it's true! It's true! It's true!"

The man sitting beside her said, "What do you mean, 'It's true'?"

"I've always been told people look like ants from a plane."

"Lady," the man said, "those are ants. We haven't taken off yet."

Giants can look like ants from God's perspective. To stimulate courage, we must look from God's perspective and purpose.

We must look at it from God's purpose. God has a purpose for problems and giants. Look at what happened with Caleb. Here is an understanding of God's purpose for going into Canaan and conquering the possessions He has for us.

"Then Moses and Aaron fell on their faces in the presence of all of the assembly of the congregation of the sons of Israel. Joshua, the son of Nun, and Caleb, the son of Jephunneh, of those who had spied out the land, tore their clothes; and they spoke to all the congregation of the sons of Israel, saying, 'The land which we passed through to spy out is exceedingly good land. [8]If the Lord is pleased with us, then He will bring us into this land and give it to us—a land which flows with milk and honey. Only do not rebel against the Lord; and do not fear the people of the land, for they shall be our prey. Their protection has been removed from them, and the Lord is with us; do not fear them.' But all the congregation said to stone them with stones. Then the glory of the Lord appeared in the tent of meeting to all of the sons of Israel" (Numbers 14:5-9).

The King James version of the Bible reads, "These giants are bread for us." The New American Standard version reads, "The giants are prey for us."

Giants are the food of champions. They are the food that makes us strong and courageous and gives us faith. They are the food that helps us understand how big God is.

While we're facing it, He is building up our faith and character. We will be better people for learning to walk with

God during these times. God wants to turn burdens into blessings. He wants to build us up in the most holy faith. You know the phrase already—if there were never a battle, there would never be a victory. Without the valleys, there are no mountains. God gives us balance in our Christian life. Regardless of what we are facing, God is bigger than our giants.

When we are facing the toughest problems we have ever faced, God wants to walk with us through all these things.

We must look at God's promise. The Word of God contains more than 9,000 promises. Caleb was claiming the promises of God. Sometimes we fail to keep our word, but God never fails to keep His word. Israel was afraid to take God at His word. God did not want them to stay longer in the wilderness but to go into the Promised Land. Because they would not see the situation through God's perspective, purpose, and promise, they died in the wilderness.

Let us make up our minds that not only are some going in but every one of us is also going in. I like what Moses said to Pharaoh when he was getting ready to bring the people out: not one person or one of their herd was going to be left behind. Not only was every man and woman leaving, but all their children, herds, and other possessions were also exiting. The Lord was going to lead them out of bondage and into a land of freedom, all for the glory of God.

Survey the challenges. Stimulate your courage. Finally, if we want to have a mountain in our heart, we must secure our conquest.

WE MUST SECURE OUR CONQUEST

How did Caleb live for forty years in the wilderness and keep a mountain in his heart? Despite these years of wandering, bickering, complaining, fussing and fighting around him, he kept the picture of the mountain alive in his heart. The older some Christians get, the faster their dreams die. They are less motivated and less determined until finally they say they are going to settle down and let younger people take over. You will not find approval for this anywhere in the Word of God. Caleb was 85 years old when he finally possessed his possession (Joshua 14:6-12).

The sons of Judah drew near to Joshua in Gilgal, and Caleb the son of Jephunneh the Kenizzite said, "You know the word which the LORD spoke to Moses the man of God concerning you and me in Kadesh-Barnea.

"I was forty years old when Moses the servant of the LORD sent me from Kadesh-Barnea to spy out the land, and I brought word back to him as it was in my heart.

"Nevertheless my brethren who went up with me made the heart of the people melt with fear; but I followed the LORD my God fully.

"So Moses swore on that day, saying, 'Surely the land on which your foot has trodden shall be an inheritance to you and to your children forever, because you have followed the LORD my God fully.'

"Now behold, the Lord has let me live, just as He spoke, these forty-five years, from the time that the LORD spoke this word to Moses, when Israel walked in the wilderness; and now behold, I am eighty-five years old today.

"I am still as strong today as I was in the day Moses sent me; as my strength was then, so my strength is now, for war and for going out and coming in.

"Now then, give me this hill country about which the LORD spoke on that day, for you heard on that day that Anakim were there, with great fortified cities; perhaps the LORD will be with me, and I will drive them out as the LORD has spoken."

At age 85, Caleb said that for forty years he had maintained a dream that he would someday possess his mountain. He said he was as strong now as the day he first saw it. He was ready to take the hill country and all the fortified cities. He believed God would give him the victory. It is time for us to make up our minds that we are going to secure our conquests. How do we do it?

We must have an undying faith. Caleb had an undying faith. He did not let the wilderness take away his mountain. A lot of people allow their emotional, mental, and physical conditions to determine what is going to happen around them. Remember what Sir Edmund said, the battle is inward, not outward. First, we need to get a mountain in our heart. Next, we need to make up our minds that God will bring the victory.

When God says it is time to go, we must go in the expectation that He will give us our mountain and perform miracles, if necessary, to make His promises a reality.

Regardless of what happens in your marriage, your school, or your church, God will fulfill His Word. If you want to have the touch of God upon your life, you must have the mountain, the dream, the vision in your heart.

Nothing is impossible for God Almighty. We need an undying faith and an unqualified devotion in our hearts.

We must have an unqualified devotion in our hearts. Caleb said he had fully served the Lord and had given his best to God all his life. We cannot have one foot on the mountain and the other in the wilderness. We cannot have one foot in the church and the other in the world. We cannot have one foot in the Spirit and the other in the flesh. We cannot be a Canaan-conqueror and a wilderness-wanderer at the same time. We cannot expect to conquer our mountain if we are halfhearted and slothful in our commitment and dedication to the Lord. It will require a complete and total surrender of our lives every day. We must have an undying faith and an unqualified devotion to God.

We must have an unending strength. It is amazing that an 85-year-old man, Caleb, was ready for war. As Christians, we too are in a spiritual war—a war for the souls of men and women. We must see mighty miracles happen. If we plan to exit the wilderness, cross the Jordan, and possess the promises of God, we are going to have to wage war with the enemy of our souls.

At 85, Caleb climbed and conquered his mountain. He did what God had put in his heart. Regardless of your age, God wants to help you reach the mountain that is in your heart. The mountains standing in the way of hurting families or jobs or financial situations or spiritual matters need to be conquered. Do not let your mountain die regardless of where you are right now. Make up your mind that you are going to conquer it in the strength and might of Jesus Christ. God is looking for people who will say, "Lord, give me that mountain."

Keep a mountain in your heart and do not let anyone take away that dream.

CONCLUSION:
The Greatest Loss In A Man's Life

On May 29, 1953, Edmund Hillary attempted to climb Mount Everest, the highest mountain on earth at 29,151 feet. He did not accomplish the feat the first time he tried. A short time afterward, someone asked him how it felt to fail in climbing that mountain. He said, "Mount Everest has grown as tall as it's ever going to grow, but I am still growing." One year later, he became the first man to climb to the top of Mount Everest. Why? He had a mountain in his heart.

On one occasion, Jesus was teaching. Mark's Gospel records these words. "And He summoned the crowd with His Disciples and said to them, 'If anyone wishes to come after me he must deny himself, take up his cross, and follow Me. For whosoever wishes to save his life will lose it, but whosoever loses his life for my sake and the Gospel will save it. And what does it profit a man to gain the whole world and forfeit his soul? For what will a man give in exchange for his soul? And whoever is ashamed of Me and My words in this adulterous and sinful generation, the Son of Man will also be ashamed of him when He comes in the glory of His Father with the Holy Angels" (Mark 8:34-38).

Have you ever pondered what it would mean if your soul should be lost? Have you ever thought about the cost, the price of what it would be to lose your soul? I rejoice with Christ followers. I weep for those who are not following Jesus Christ. Jesus talks about a loss that is beyond comprehension.

You might be one of those people who window-shops at the jewelry store when you are in a shopping mall. Some people just like to admire the diamonds in those glass cases. We would not think of a person spending more time taking care of the diamond.

Let the diamond represent your soul and your body represent the glass case. The case is not nearly as important as the diamond. When God created you, He created you as a living soul and that soul lives inside a box we call the body.

Many people become more concerned about the box than the diamond. Think about it. Look at what people do. They feed the box, they rest the box, they bathe the box, they scratch the box, they sleep the box. In short, we spend some amount of time to take care of the box. However, many men are in danger of losing the diamond while taking care of the box. They may feed the box only from fast food restaurants, but they spend even less time on the diamond inside.

What is life's greatest loss? Jesus said, "What would it profit a man to gain the whole world and lose his own soul?" The most important chapter in this entire book is where are you going to spend eternity. How do you know that you're saved and you're ready to go and meet the Heavenly Father and give an account of your life?

THE VALUE OF YOUR SOUL

First, understand *the value of your soul.* Your soul is valuable because of its *workmanship.* God made it. Have you ever thought about a soul? What does it look like? What does it weigh? How do you describe it? What is it? Think about it. We can describe many things in this world, but it's very hard to describe our soul. Have you ever seen it? Can you describe it? And yet, you have one, and so do I.

Many people are willing to exchange what they cannot see for the things they see. They're willing to change the things that are priceless for the things that are passing away. The Bible says that we are "fearfully and wonderfully made." The Bible says that we are "body, soul, and spirit."

Your soul is valuable because of its *workmanship*. Your soul is valuable because of its *durability*. Your soul will be in existence after this earth has passed away.

How long is eternity?

---

*Man, in his finite mind, has tried to grasp the
length of eternity.*

One of the best ways I've come to understand is through the following metaphor. Imagine a seagull walking along the beach, let's say the Atlantic seaboard. The seagull reaches down with his beak and picks up one grain of sand. He flies all the way to the west coast and deposits that one grain of sand. Then he picks up one grain of sand from the Pacific coast and flies all the way back to the Atlantic seashore and deposits that one grain of sand. Some two thousand miles each way, four thousand miles total. I don't know how long it would take that seagull to fly to the Pacific and then all the way back to the Atlantic, but imagine with me that that bird went back and forth, back and forth, back and forth, back and forth, until one day in the future all the grains of sand that used to be on the Atlantic seaboard are now all the way on the Pacific seaboard, and all the grains of sand that used to be on the Pacific beaches are now on the Atlantic beaches. Once that seagull had accomplished that great feat, eternity would not even be one second long.

Your soul will be in existence when the heavens roll up like a scroll. Your soul will be in existence when the Earth melts with a fervent heat. Your soul will be in existence when we pass from this life to the next.

Your soul is valuable because of its *durability*. Your soul is valuable because of its *cost*. Your soul is valuable because Jesus died for it. You're not redeemed by corruptible things like silver and gold but with the precious blood of the Lord Jesus Christ. With the silver of His tears and the gold of His blood, He paid the price to give you eternal life. Our soul is valuable because Jesus Christ paid for it.

In our world, real estate is up and down, the economy is up and down, merchandise is up and down, all based upon the price that people are willing to pay for it. But the value of your soul is worth more than all the wealth of the world.

How valuable is your soul? I will tell you. If you climb up to Heaven and put your ear on the beating heart of God you will hear God's heartbeat for your soul. Then climb down to the bloody slopes of Calvary and look at the Son of God hanging, enduring the agony of crucifixion. He is dying for your soul. The Lord Jesus experienced Hell for three days for your soul. Then see Jesus as He comes out of the grave to give us Heaven and happiness for eternity. That's how valuable your soul is. Your soul is valuable because Jesus paid for it.

Your *soul is valuable because of its rareness*. There is only one of you. There is no other person exactly like you. You are the handiwork of God. You are one of a kind. There are seven billion people on this planet today, and not one of them is like you. There is no one else like you, yet the Lord knows you by name. He knows the number of hairs on your head. He knows every thought in your mind. He knows every aspect of you. Your soul is valuable because of its rareness. There's no one else like you. You may have an identical twin brother, but just because there are two of you doesn't mean there is a lack of uniqueness in you. When Jesus Christ died, He died just for you. If you had been the only one on the Earth at the time of redemption, He would have died just for you.

The value of your soul; *your soul is valuable because of its workmanship,* because of its *durability, because of its cost, and because of its rareness.*

THE VANITY OF THE WORLD

Jesus said, "What does it profit a man if he should gain the wealth of the whole world and lose his own soul?" Jesus contrasted the vanity of the world with the value of the soul. Some people get a bad bargain in exchange for their souls. No one person has ever gained the whole world. People have tried it. Every one of them has failed. Empires have arisen. Empires have come crashing down. Armies have marched across the world, trying to conquer, trying to own it, to their own demise, only to see it fall apart.

It is amazing how cheaply people will sell Jesus. Judas sold Him for thirty pieces of silver. There are people who will sell Him to get a bus ticket. There are people who will sell Him to get a new job. It's amazing how people will grasp for the things of this world.

Not only has no one ever gained the whole world, but no one keeps what they gain. There is not one person in this world who has ever taken the wealth that they have accumulated to glory. This world is passing away and everything in it. As one preacher put it, "Where some of you are going, it would melt when you got there!"

There has never been a person, rich or poor, who took what he owned to glory. He left it all behind. The man who strives to accumulate more wealth for the sake of wealth's sake, one day will be greatly disappointed, because he will leave it all. It will all pass away.

Not only can you not gain it, you can't keep it, but also, this world will never satisfy you.

People try to find satisfaction in many things that are passing away. But real satisfaction is found in Jesus and Him alone. You were made for God. Your inner heart will never be satisfied until you give your heart to Jesus. If you're trying to find satisfaction in this world, you will never find it.

What did God make a fish to do? He made a fish to swim in the sea. What did God make a bird to do? He made a bird to fly in the air. If you take a fish out of the sea and put him in a tree, he'll be a very unhappy fish. If you take a bird out of the air and make him swim in the sea, he'll be an unhappy bird. And why did God make you? He made you to have fellowship with Him.

God made you so that you could know Him, and you will never be satisfied until you do. You'll be like a fish in a tree, like a bird in the sea. You'll never find satisfaction or fulfillment until Christ is the Lord of your life.

When we are not walking with Christ, there's darkness in our hearts. There's only one way to get that darkness out of our hearts. We cannot educate it out. We can't think it out. We can't sweat it out. We can't just believe it out. There's only one way that the darkness will get out of our hearts, and that is by allowing the light of the Gospel to come in. When Christ comes into the heart, the darkness in the heart automatically goes.

It's not that man has a darkness problem. It's that man has a light problem. When we allow the light of the Gospel,

Jesus Christ Himself, to come into our hearts, we won't have a darkness problem. Christ wants to conquer all that is within us. When sin is on the throne of our hearts, our lives are in chaos and life doesn't make sense any more. When Christ is on the throne of our hearts, our lives are well.

It is a bad bargain to sell one's soul for the world because we can't gain the world, we can't keep the world, and what we do get of it won't satisfy us.

Many years ago, the grave and throne were discovered that had belonged to Charlemagne, the former King of France. He reigned centuries ago in France. When they found him, Charlemagne was still sitting on his throne. All that was there was his bony skeleton. Sitting on his knee was a Bible. His finger bone was sitting on a verse, and the verse was the verse that is the text of our chapter. "What should it profit a man to gain the wealth of the whole world and lose his own soul?"

Charlemagne had tried to conquer the then-known world and couldn't keep it. He lost it and it didn't satisfy. I wonder if he had the opportunity again, what would he do?

You still have an opportunity. I'm thrilled that you took the time to read this book about life's greatest questions, but you will never know fulfillment, you will never know satisfaction until Jesus Christ is the Lord of your life.

THE VASTNESS OF THE LOST

Have you really thought about what would happen if you were to be lost? He said, "What would it profit a man to gain the whole world and *lose* his soul?" Have you thought about what that loss would be like?

If you lose your soul, *it is an irreplaceable loss.* You can replace some things, but you cannot replace your soul. If your car is stolen, you can buy another car. If your house burns down, it is possible to build another house. If you lose something precious to you, it is possible that you can replace it or get something similar. But when you lose your soul, it is forever, and forever and forever. It is irreplaceable. There is no way you can obtain another soul once your soul has been lost. It is an irreplaceable loss.

And, *it is an irreversible loss*. When you die in this world without Jesus Christ in your heart, there is no chance of making things right. There is no chance of making Heaven. If you want mercy, you can have it, but you must have it now. If you want forgiveness, you can have it, but you must have it now. The Bible says, "It is appointed to man once to die and then the Judgment." If you want mercy, if you want forgiveness, you can have it, but you must have it now.

There's no such thing upon your death that you'll ever have the opportunity to make things right again.

There's no such thing as reincarnation where you come back as something else with another opportunity to get to a higher level of existence. It is an irreplaceable loss.

It is also an immeasurable loss. There's no way to measure your loss if you were to die and your soul be lost forever. The Bible says your soul is worth more than all the wealth of the world. The Bible says that your soul is worth more than all the precious jewels and riches and economies that this Earth could ever put together. It is an immeasurable loss. What are you trying to gain in exchange for the loss of your soul? What are you willing to exchange for it?

Let's think about it for a moment. Would you be willing to lose one thumb for the wealth of the world? You'd probably say, "Well, sure. Cut my thumb off for all the gold in the world." Would you do it for a hand, for all the wealth in the world? You might say, "Sure, cut my hand off for all the diamonds that this world has to offer." But would you do it for two hands? Would you cut off both hands? Somebody might do that for all the gold, silver, and platinum of this world. There are some men who would be willing to do that.

How about two hands and a foot? How about two hands and two feet? There are not many men who would think the wealth of this world would be worth the loss of two hands and both feet. How about two hands, both feet and one ear?

How about both ears? I don't know anyone who would be willing to lose both hands, both feet and both ears. I don't know of one man who would say that the wealth of this world is worth all that.

But think of this. If you die without Jesus Christ in your heart, it is a greater loss than losing both ears, both eyes, both hands and both feet. You would not think of exchanging your hands and your feet and your eyes and your ears for the wealth of the world, but yet there's so many that don't give much thought to the exchange of their soul for all the wealth of the world. It is an immeasurable loss.

There is no way that you and I could ever calculate the cost of such a loss, and yet the truth of the matter is, some are giving a whole lot more and getting a whole lot less when they lose their soul. It is an immeasurable loss.

It is an inexcusable loss. It is inexcusable for Jesus to come to Earth and die for your sins and then you to die and go to a devil's Hell because you refused to give him your heart. It is inexcusable. What would you do if someone came and offered you the opportunity and yet you refused to do so? Would you turn to God one day and say it's His fault? He didn't give you an opportunity to do so? He gave you creation above. He gave you a conscience within. He gave you crowds around you. He gave Christ who whispered to you. And yet you rejected Him as Lord and Savior. Does that really make sense?

Some time ago, there was a tragic fire in Oklahoma City. A house was burning down. A fireman with great courage rushed into that burning house because the mom and dad outside were saying, "Our daughter's inside. Our baby daughter's inside. Please, if you can, save our daughter, save our daughter."

Mom and dad watched that courageous fireman as he made his way into that burning house and into the bedroom of the child. He quickly grabbed what he thought was the baby and rushed back out. Then he realized that what he had grabbed was the doll but he had left the baby inside. The baby was consumed by the flames. I can think of only one thing more tragic than that. The thing that can be more tragic is for someone to die and go to the hot fires of Hell holding in his hands the toys of this world.

It is an indescribable loss. It is indescribable when a man fails to make Jesus Christ the Lord and Savior of his life. It is so simple and quick to do so. In a few pages, you will find out how.

The greatest loss of all would be for you to know that Jesus died for you, to know that the Gospel was for you, and to reject it.

Now allow me to ask you outright. Please, don't allow the value of your soul, the vanity of the world and the vastness of the loss to make you harden yourself against Christ. Let it soften your heart. If you know the way to know Christ as your personal savior, and yet you choose to reject him, your heart can become as hard as the concrete that your car drives on. There will never be a better opportunity to come to know Jesus Christ as your personal savior than today. Tomorrow, if you put it off, you will have more sin to confess than you do today. Tomorrow you'll have less time and more sin. And, tomorrow you'll have a harder heart. There's never a better time to get Christ to come into your heart than it is this very moment.

This is your day of salvation. This is your day of eternal life. Accept Him today. And become the man that God intended you to become.

There is a mountain in every man's heart that he cannot scale alone. The only way to move this mountain is to give your heart to Christ and let him stand on the roof of the world in your life.

———————— ❧ ————————

I close, *Scaling Your Everest,* with one of greatest missionary stories of all time. I trust it will inspire you to scale your Everest and finish what the Lord has chosen for you to be and do in this life. In 1812, Adoniram and Ann Judson left Massachusetts for India. After a brief stay in India, he and his wife traveled to Burma, arriving in 1813. They were both 24 years of age when they left America. In Burma, no one knew the English language and the Judsons learned the language on their own.

In those early years experienced the heartbreaking loss of two children. In 1822, Ann's health broke and she returned to the States for rest, publishing a book on their pioneering missionary work in Burma. Upon her return, in 1824, Adoniram was imprisoned and tortured. Ann followed her husband from prison to prison and preserved his and several others' lives by bribing officials and providing food. In 1826, after 2 years imprisonment, Adoniram was released. But in October of that same year, while Adoniram was away, Ann died at age 38, worn out from hardships.

Listen to the letter that Adoniram wrote Ann's father, when he requested her hand in marriage. "I have now to ask whether you can consent to part with your daughter early next spring, to see her no more in this world. Whether you can consent to see her departure to a heathen land, and her subjection to the hardships and sufferings of a missionary life? Whether you can consent to her exposure to the dangers of the ocean; to the fatal influence of the southern climate of India; to every kind of want and distress; to the degradation, insult, persecution, and perhaps a violent death? Can you consent to this, for the sake of the perish immortal souls, for the sake of Zion and the glory of God? Can you consent to all this, in hope of soon meeting your daughter in the world of glory, with a crown of righteousness brightened by the acclamations of praise which shall redound to her Savior from heathens saved, through her means, from eternal woe and despair?

Statistics are not clear, but it seems there were between a dozen and twenty-five enduring Burmese converts at the time of Judson's death in 1850. He was only 62. But, one mission was completed--the Burmese had the Bible in their own language--a translation that stands to this day, with over 2 million Christians in Myanmar! In succession, the three women Judson married and died before him--and he lost his life at sea.

His one surviving son, Edward, speaking at the dedication of the Judson Memorial Church in New York City, summarized his father's story: "Suffering and success go together. If you are succeeding without suffering, it is because others before you have suffered; if you are suffering without succeeding, it is that others after you may succeed." You can scale your Everest!

How to Become a Christian Man

Change Your Mind: The first step in becoming a Christian is to repent or to change your mind about Christ and sin. To repent is to have a life-altering change of mind concerning your need to live a life of obedience to God. To make a decision to come to faith in Christ that is genuine— one that will stand the test of time—you must have a sincerely remorseful, repentant heart. It has been said that *repentance* is the first word of the gospel.

Change Your Heart: All you have to do, if you're ready, is bow your head in prayer, repent by sincerely asking Jesus Christ to forgive you of all your sins, ask Him to be your Savior having paid the price for your sins through His death on the cross, and promise to be as obedient to God's will as you possibly can. It's that simple. There is no specific way to do it. There is no special prayer you have to say word for word. All it takes is a repentant heart through faith in Christ with a sincere desire to turn from your former ways and follow Christ.

If you have prayed a prayer of forgiveness and accepted Jesus Christ as your Lord and Savior, you are now ready for eternity in heaven. You are a Christian and will inherit eternal life with Christ in Heaven when you die or He returns to this earth to gather His children home. The peace of God that has filled your heart will also be your guide in the years to come. According to the Bible, you have become a new person in Christ. In the weeks ahead, old habits will pass away as you become more like Christ.

What Do I Do Now that I've Accepted Christ?

- Seek other Christians to fellowship with in a church of your choice that uses the Bible for instruction in holy living.

- Start reading the Bible regularly to get to know God better and understand His will for your life.

- Be baptized in water by immersion. If you were baptized as an infant, you need to be baptized again. Baptism is your public acknowledgement of your acceptance of Jesus Christ as your Lord and Savior. Although you can get to Heaven without being baptized, Jesus told us we should be baptized, just as He was! Follow the Lord's example and do this as soon as possible.

- Tell others about your decision to follow Christ that they may be led to follow in your footsteps. There is no greater accomplishment than to lead another person to Christ!

ABOUT THE AUTHOR

Dr. James O. Davis founded Cutting Edge International and co-founded the Billion Soul Network, a growing coalition of more than 1,500 Christian ministries and denominations synergizing their efforts to build the premier community of pastors worldwide to help plant five million new churches for a billion soul harvest. The Billion Soul Network, with more than 475,000 churches, has become the largest pastors network in the world.

Christian leaders recognize Dr. Davis as one of the leading networkers in the Christian world. More than 50,000 pastors and leaders have attended his biannual pastors conference and leadership summits across the United States and in all major world regions. He has networked with significant leaders from different spheres such as George O. Wood, Jack Hayford, Johnny Hunt, Kenneth Ulmer, David Mohan, Reinhard Bonnke, Charles Blake, James Merritt, Leonard Sweet, Barry Black, and others.

Dr. Davis served twelve years leading 1,500 evangelists and training thousands of students for full-time evangelism as the National Evangelists Representative at the Assemblies of God world headquarters. Ministering more than 45 weeks per year for almost 30 years to an average yearly audience of 150,000 people, Dr. Davis has now traveled nearly eight million miles to minister face-to-face to more than 6 million people in more than 110 nations.

Dr. Davis earned a Doctorate in Ministry in Preaching at Trinity Evangelical Divinity School and two master's degrees from the Assemblies of God Theological Seminary. As an author and editor, he has provided: *How To Make Your Net Work: Tying Relational Knots For Global Impact; The Pastor's Best Friend: The New Testament Evangelist; Living Like Jesus; The Preacher's Summit; Gutenberg to Google:*

The Twenty Indispensable Laws of Communication, What To Do When The Lights Go Out, It's a Miraculous Life! and *Signposts On The Road To Armageddon.* With Dr. Bill Bright, he co-authored *Beyond All Limits: The Synergistic Church for a Planet in Crisis.* His quotes and articles have appeared in *Charisma, Ministry Today, The Challenge Weekly, New York Times Magazine,* and elsewhere.

Dr. Davis resides in the Orlando area with his wife, Sheri, and daughters, Olivia and Priscilla. They have two children, Jennifer and James, who reside in heaven.

James O. Davis may be invited to speak for your church or organization by contacting:

James O. Davis
P. O. Box 411605
Melbourne, Florida 32941-1605
(417) 861-9999
www.JamesODavis.com

MORE DYNAMIC BOOKS

by Dr. James O. Davis

What to Do When the Lights Go Out

The Pastor's Best Friend

Living Like Jesus

Twelve Big Ideas

Gutenberg to Google:
The Twenty Indispensable Laws of Communication

Signposts to Armageddon: The Road to Eternity

It's a Miraculous Life!

Beyond All Limits:
The Synergistic Church for a Planet in Crisis

How To Make Your Net Work:
Tying Relational Knots For Global Impact

If this book has ministered to you, please prayerfully consider giving monthly support to Cutting Edge International at www.JamesODavis.com. Those who provide monthly support receive a FREE copy of each new book that Dr. Davis releases.

To learn more about walking with Jesus Christ, or for more information about the author and for additional resources that will strengthen your walk with Jesus Christ, please visit us online at www.JamesODavis.com.

MAJORING IN MEN® CURRICULUM

MANHOOD GROWTH PLAN

"One of the main reasons the Billion Soul Network exists in the global Church is to discover the finest resources and to make Christians aware of them everywhere. As I have traveled and taught worldwide, I know Edwin Louis Cole's Majoring in Men® Curriculum is the finest men's training and most widely-used curriculum for men in the world. Start learning today with the following books and workbooks to power up legendary manhood!" ~ James O. Davis

Order the corresponding workbook for each book, and study the first four Majoring In Men® Curriculum books in this order:

MAXIMIZED MANHOOD: Realize your need for God in every area of your life and start mending relationships with Christ and your family.

COURAGE: Make peace with your past, learn the power of forgiveness and the value of character. Let yourself be challenged to speak up for Christ to other men.

COMMUNICATION, SEX AND MONEY: Increase your ability to communicate, place the right values on sex and money in relationships, and greatly improve relationships, whether married or single.

STRONG MEN IN TOUGH TIMES: Reframe trials, battles and discouragement in light of Scripture and gain solid footing for business, career, and relational choices in the future.

Choose five of the following books to study next. When you have completed nine books, if you are not in men's group, you can find a Majoring In Men® group near you and become "commissioned" to minister to other men.

DARING: Overcome fear to live a life of daring ambition for Godly pursuits.

SEXUAL INTEGRITY: Recognize the sacredness of the sexual union, overcome mistakes and blunders and commit to righteousness in your sexuality.

THE UNIQUE WOMAN: Discover what makes a woman tick, from adolescence through maturity, to be able to minister to a spouse's uniqueness at any age.

NEVER QUIT: Take the ten steps for entering or leaving any situation, job, relationship or crisis in life.

REAL MAN: Discover the deepest meaning of Christlikeness and learn to exercise good character in times of stress, success or failure.

POWER OF POTENTIAL: Start making solid business and career choices based on Biblical principles while building core character that affects your entire life.

ABSOLUTE ANSWERS: Adopt practical habits and pursue Biblical solutions to overcome "prodigal problems" and secret sins that hinder both success and satisfaction with life.

TREASURE: Practice Biblical solutions and principles on the job to find treasures such as the satisfaction of exercising integrity and a job well done.

IRRESISTIBLE HUSBAND: Avoid common mistakes that sabotage a relationship and learn simple solutions and good habits to build a marriage that will consistently increase in intensity for decades.

MAJORING IN MEN® CURRICULUM

CHURCH GROWTH PLAN
STRONG - SUSTAINABLE - SYNERGISTIC

THREE PRACTICAL PHASES TO A POWERFUL MEN'S MOVEMENT IN YOUR CHURCH

Phase One:
- Pastor disciples key men/men's director using Maximized Manhood system.
- Launch creates momentum among men
- Church becomes more attractive to hold men who visit
- Families grow stronger
- Men increase bond to pastor

Phase Two:
- Men/men's director teach other men within the church
- Increased tithing and giving by men
- Decreased number of families in crisis
- Increased mentoring of teens and children
- Increase of male volunteers
- Faster assimilation for men visitors - clear path for pastor to connect with new men
- Men pray regularly for pastor

Phase Three:
- Men teach other men outside the church and bring them to Christ
- Increased male population and attraction to a visiting man, seeing a place he belongs
- Stronger, better-attended community outreaches
- Men are loyal to and support pastor

This system enables the pastor to successfully train key leaders, create momentum, build a church that attracts and holds men who visit, and disciple strong men.

Churches may conduct men's ministry entirely
free of charge! Learn how by calling 817-437-4888